© 2022 by ADISAN Publishing AB, Sweden

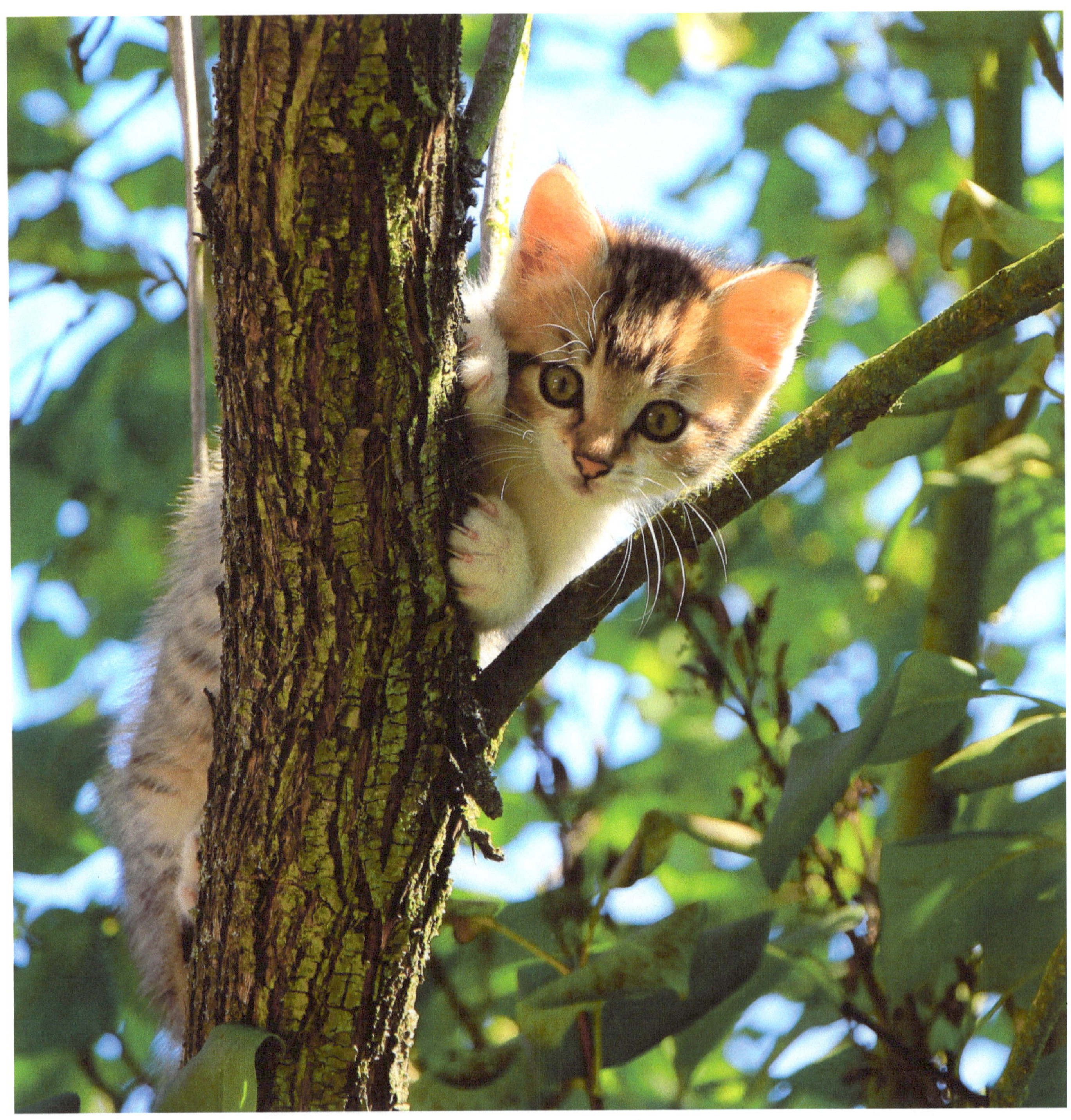

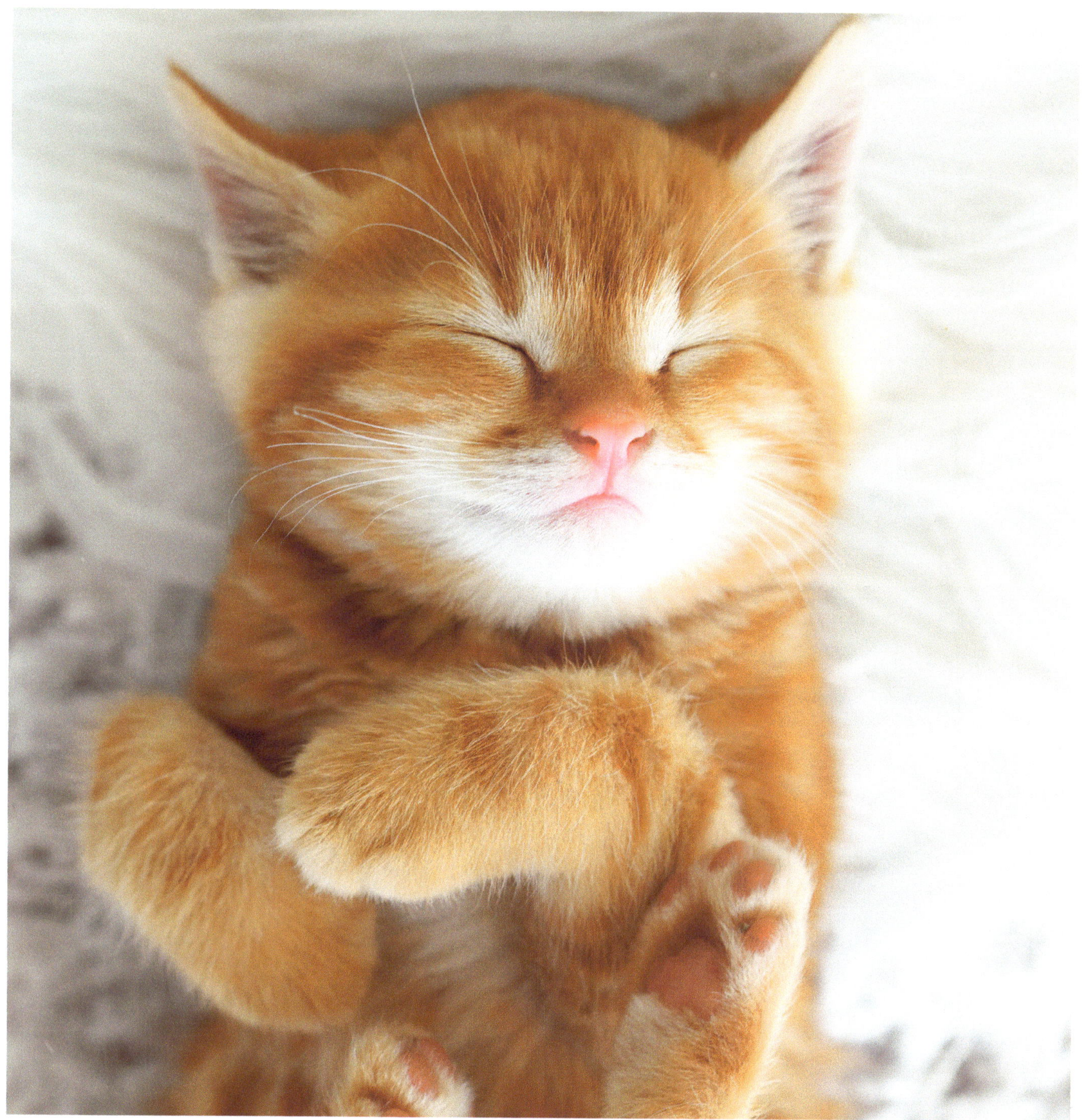

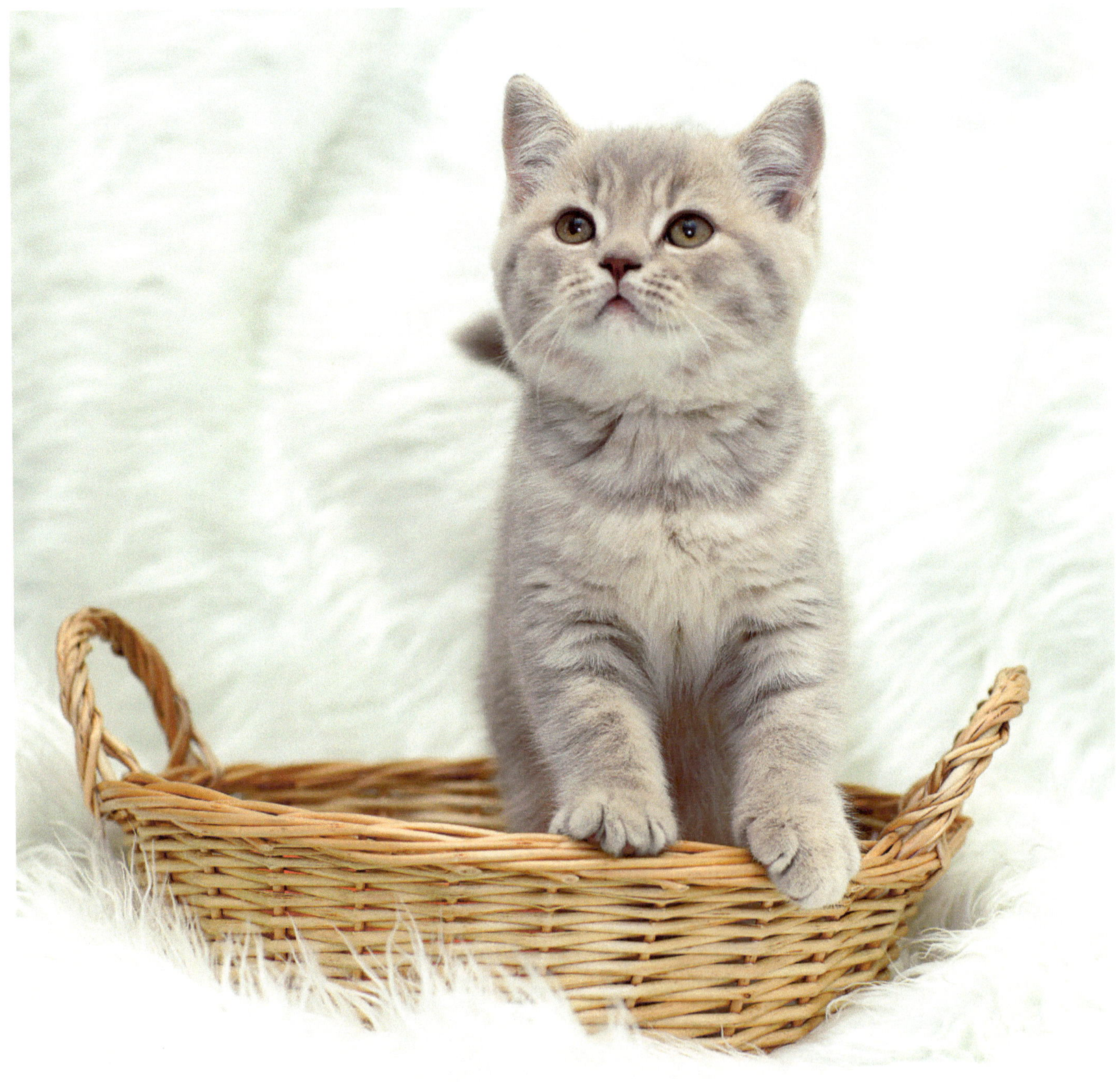

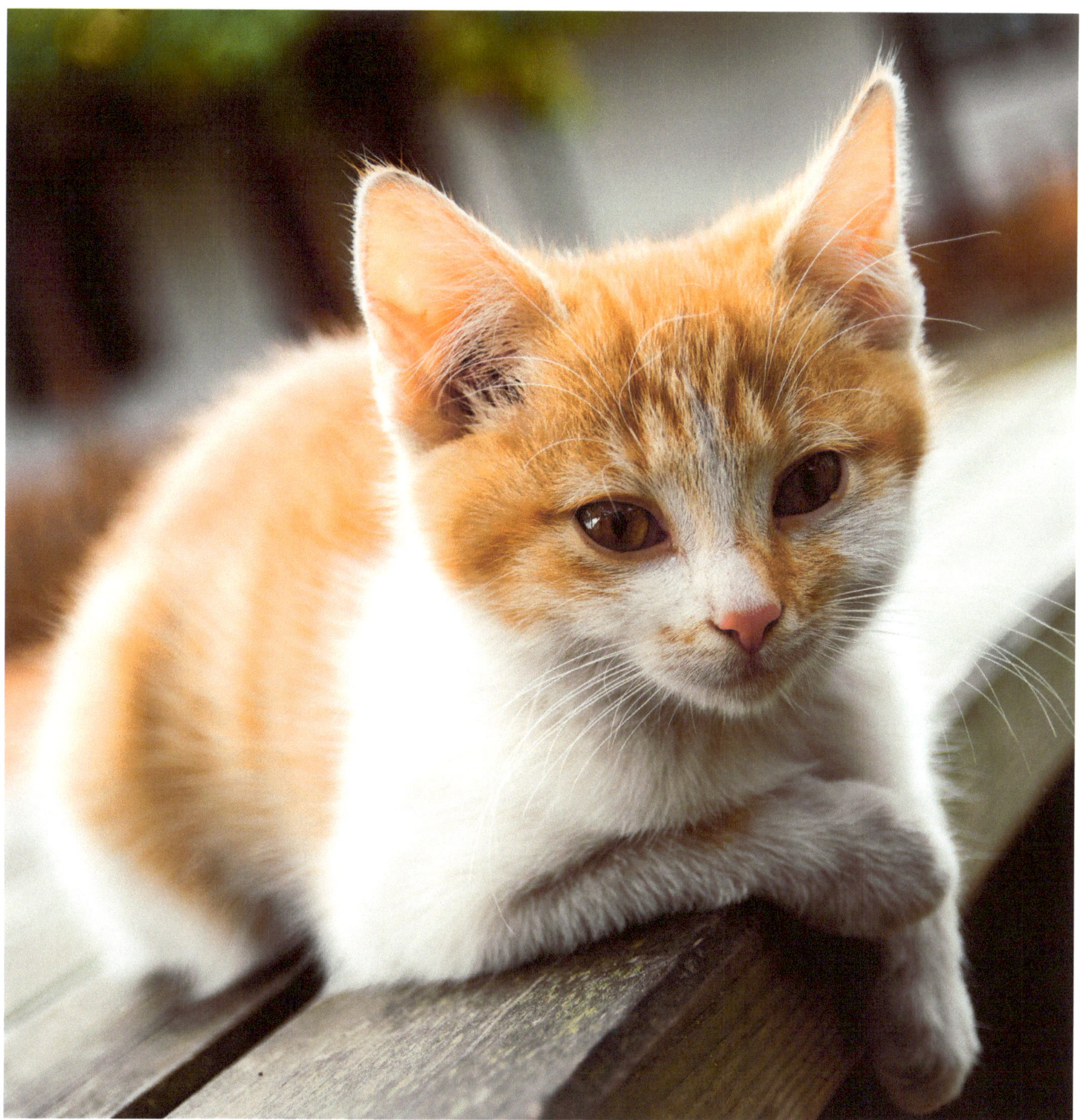

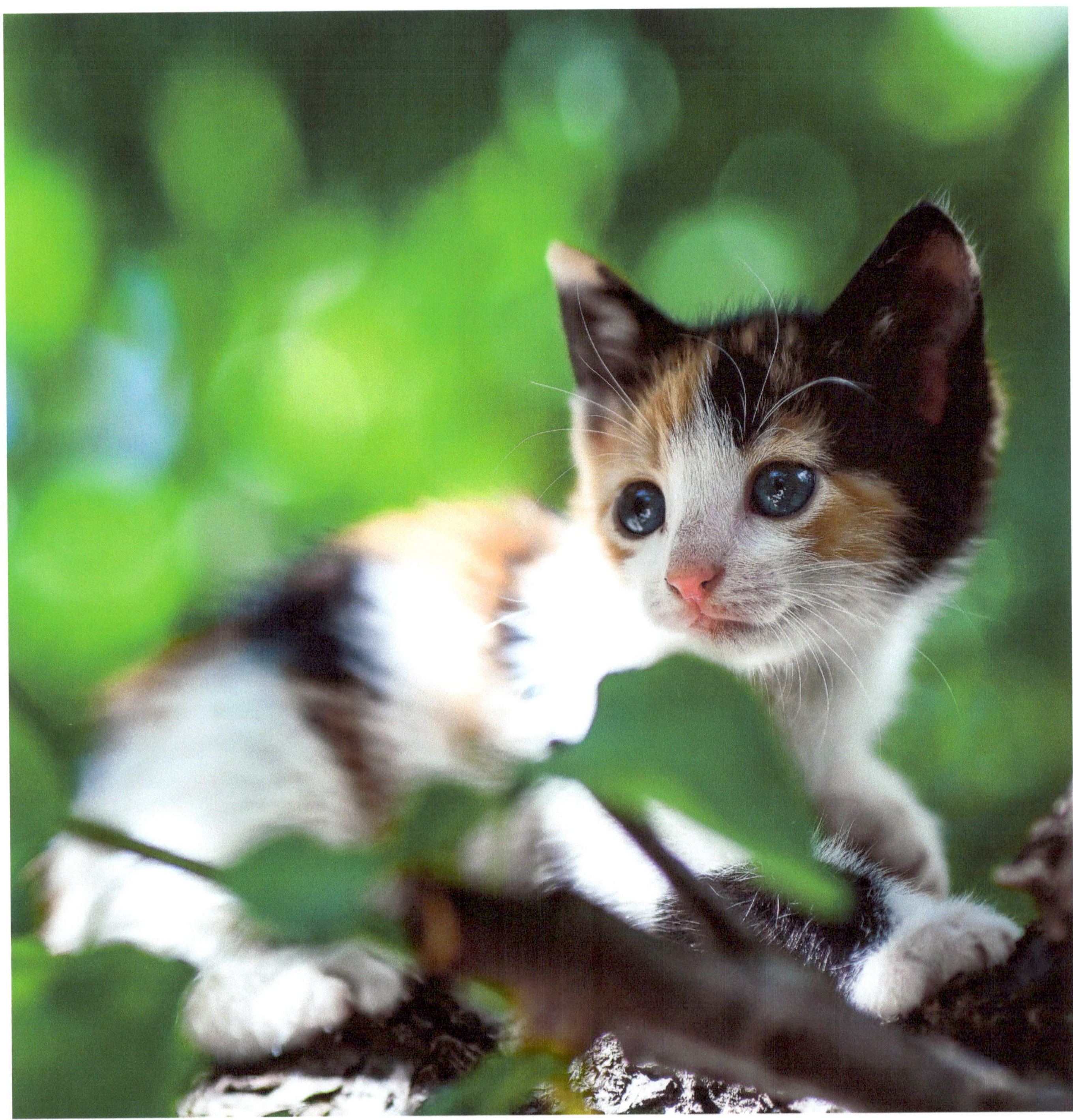

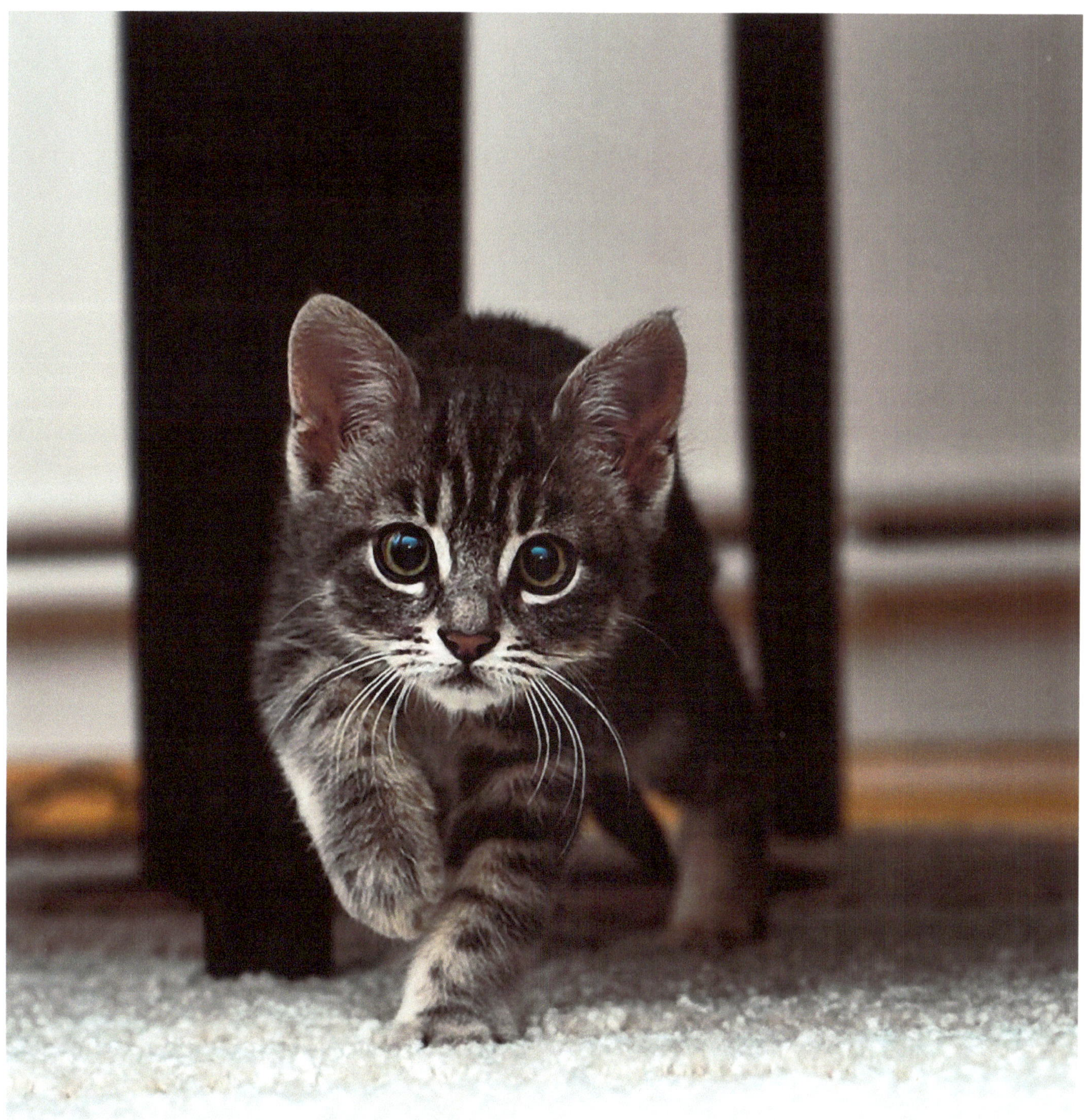

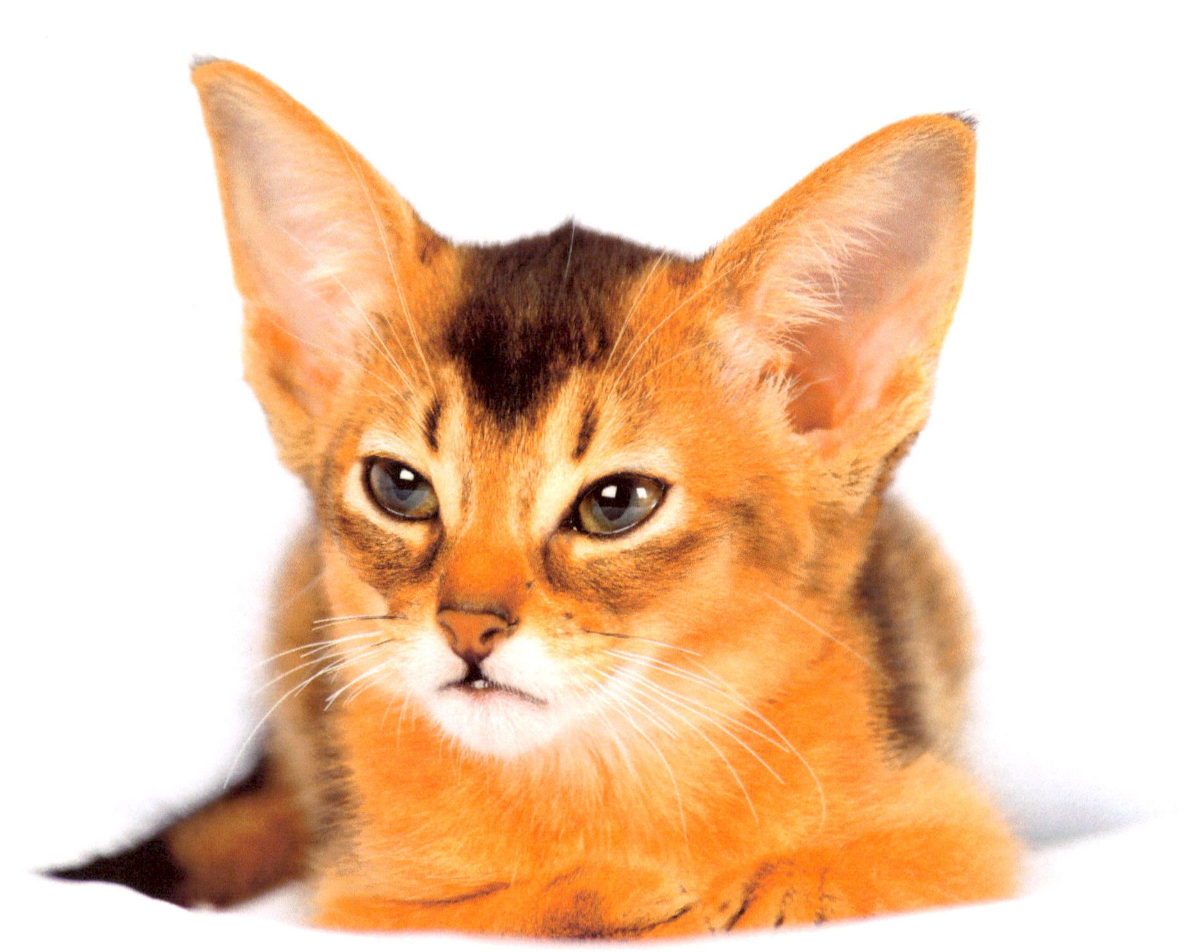

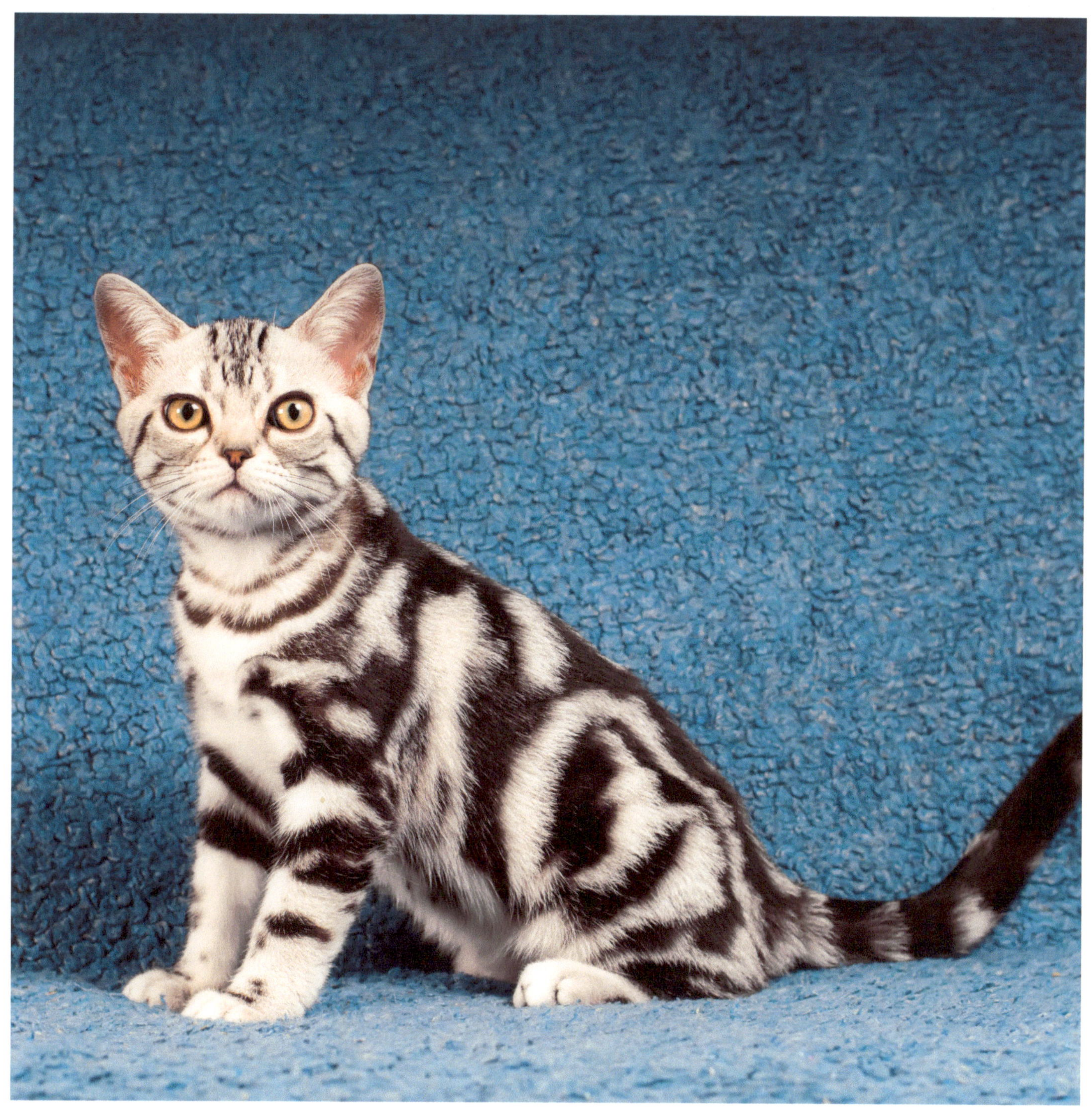

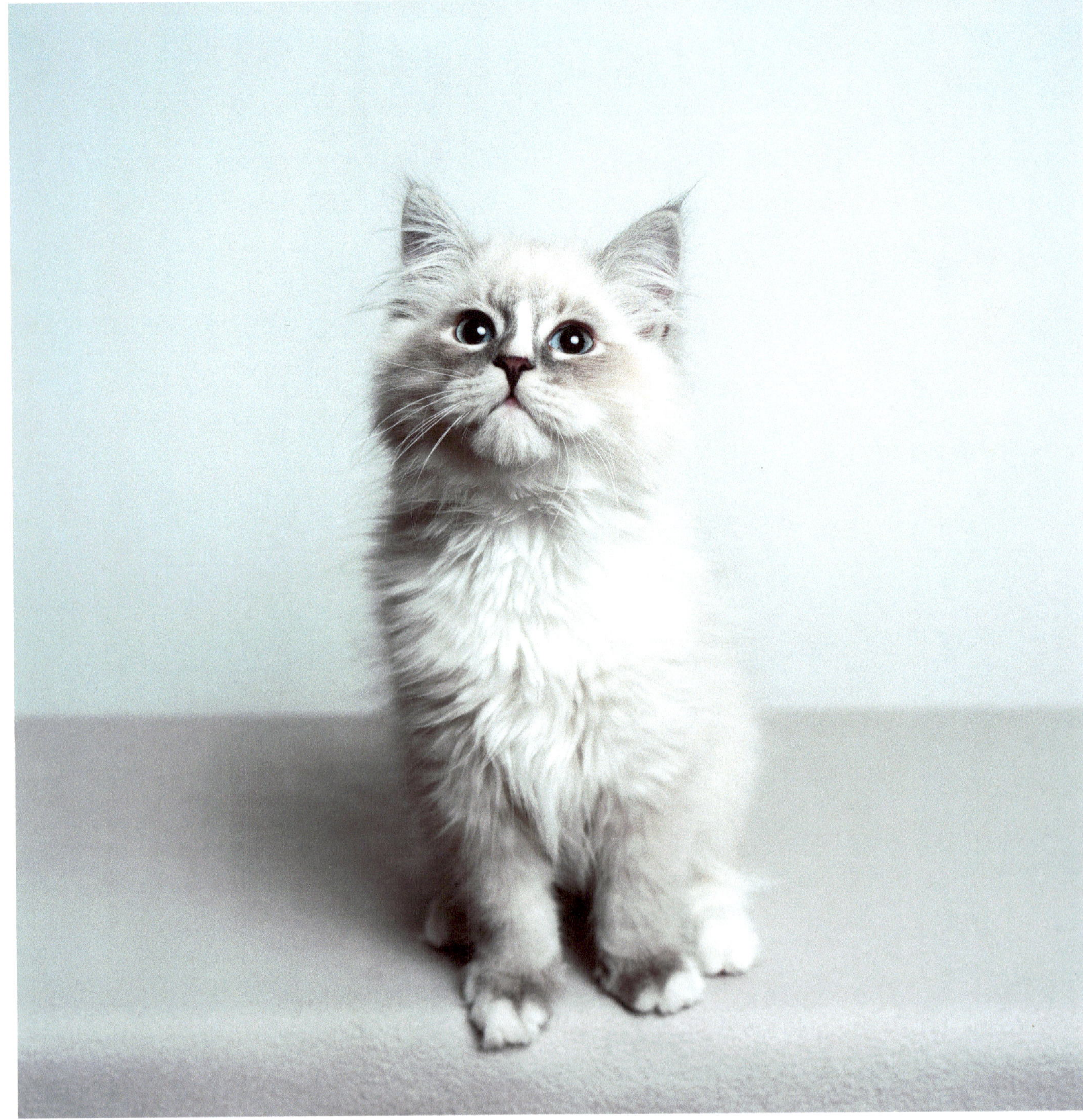

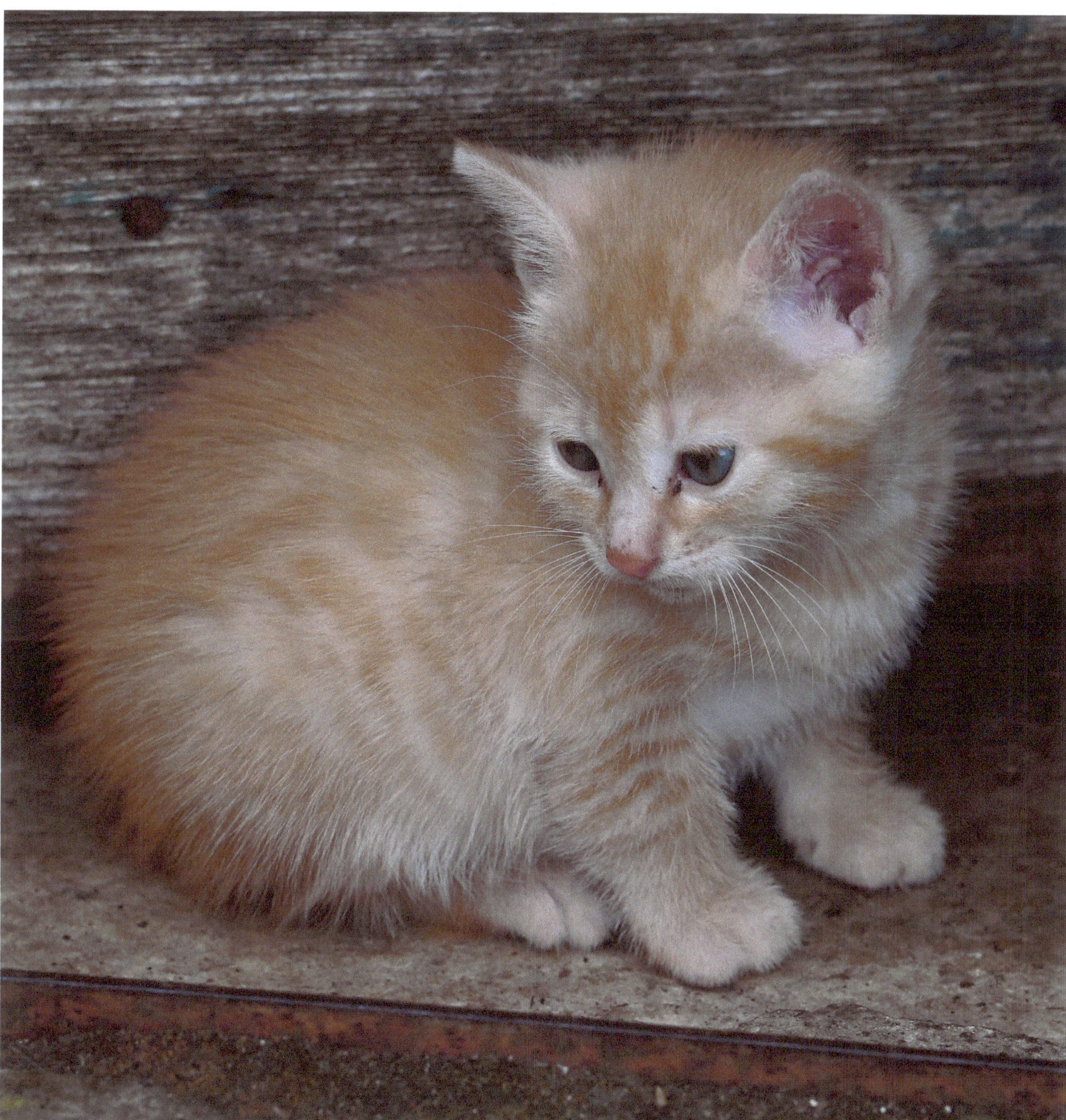

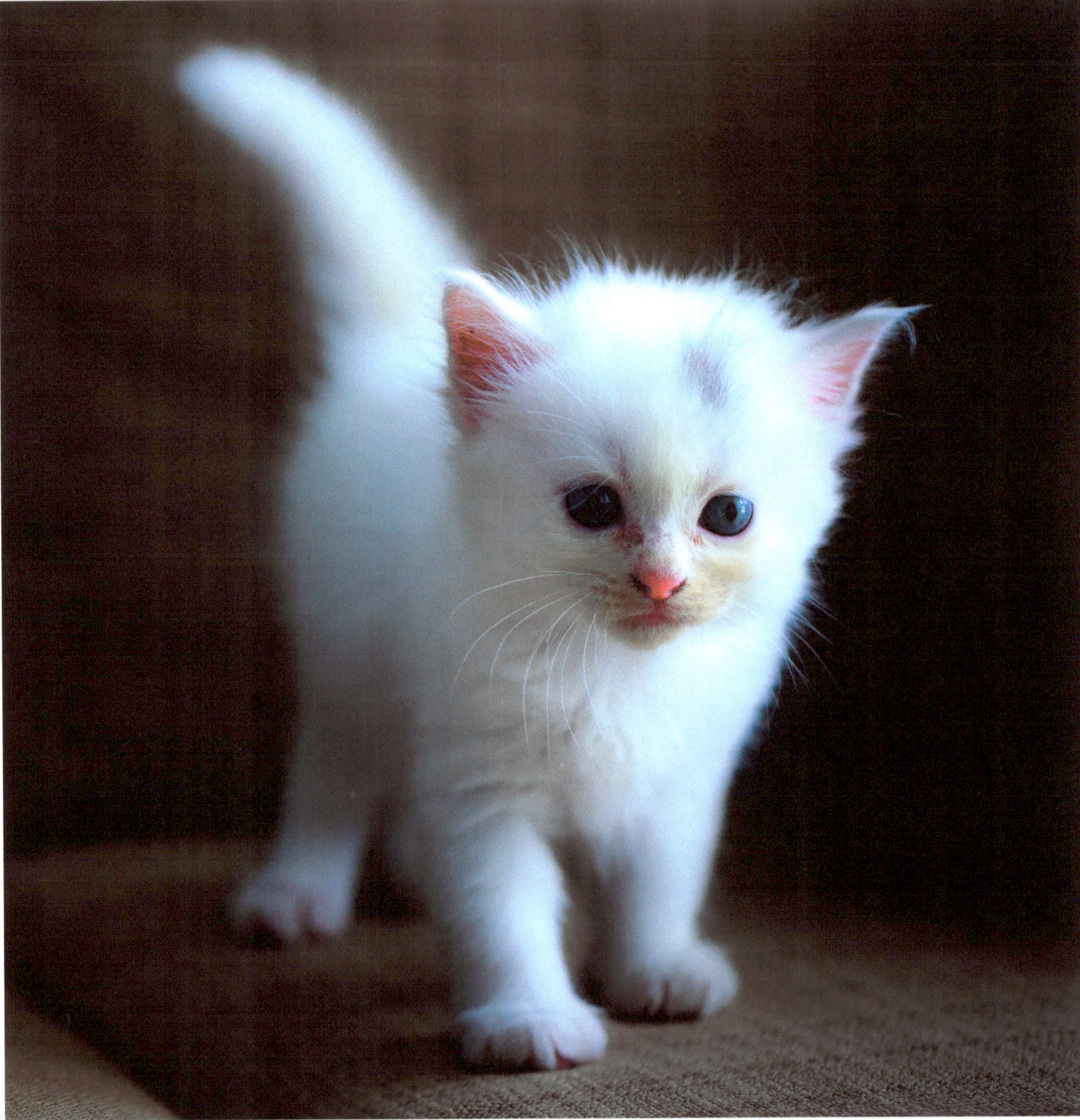

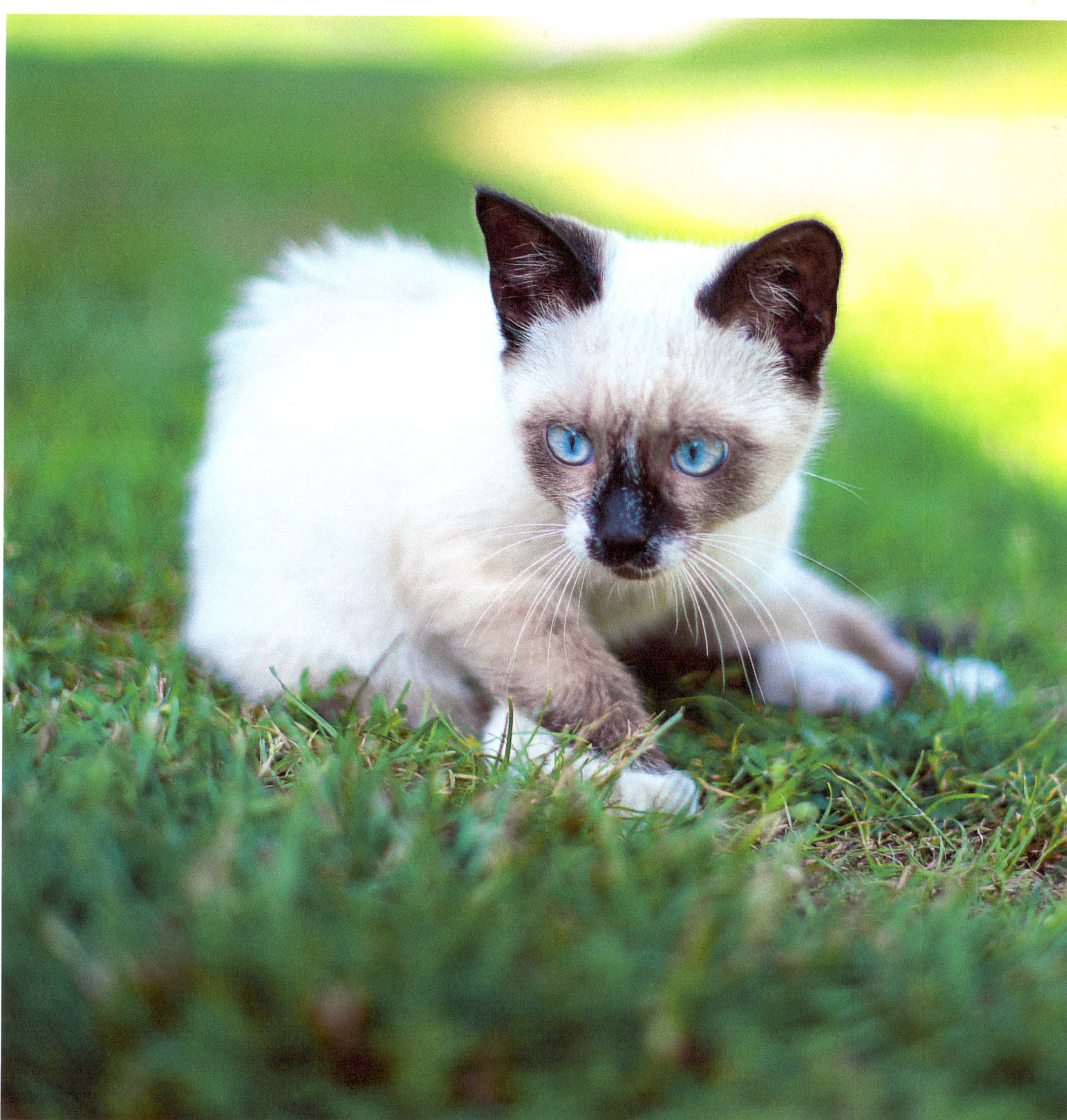

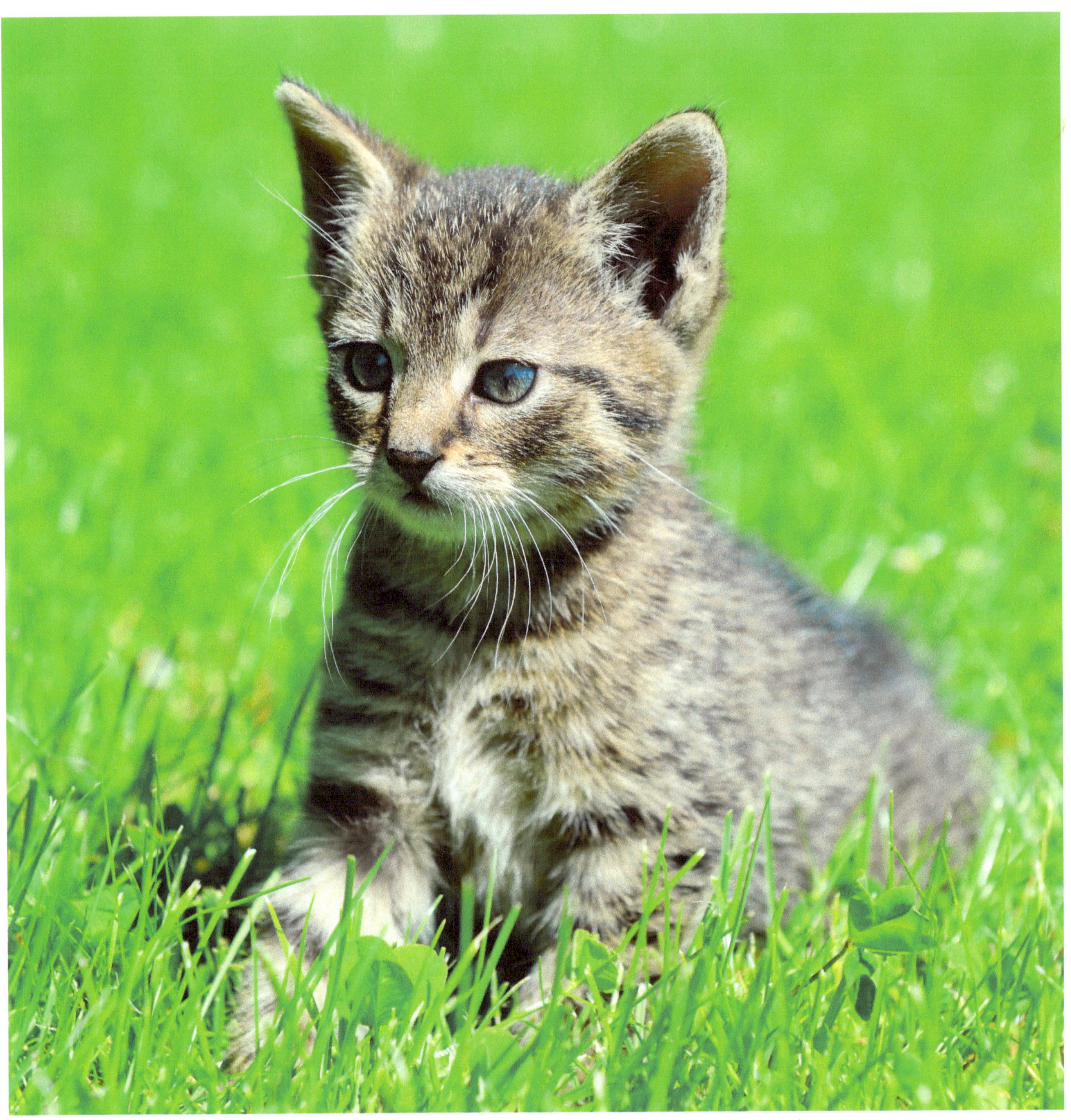

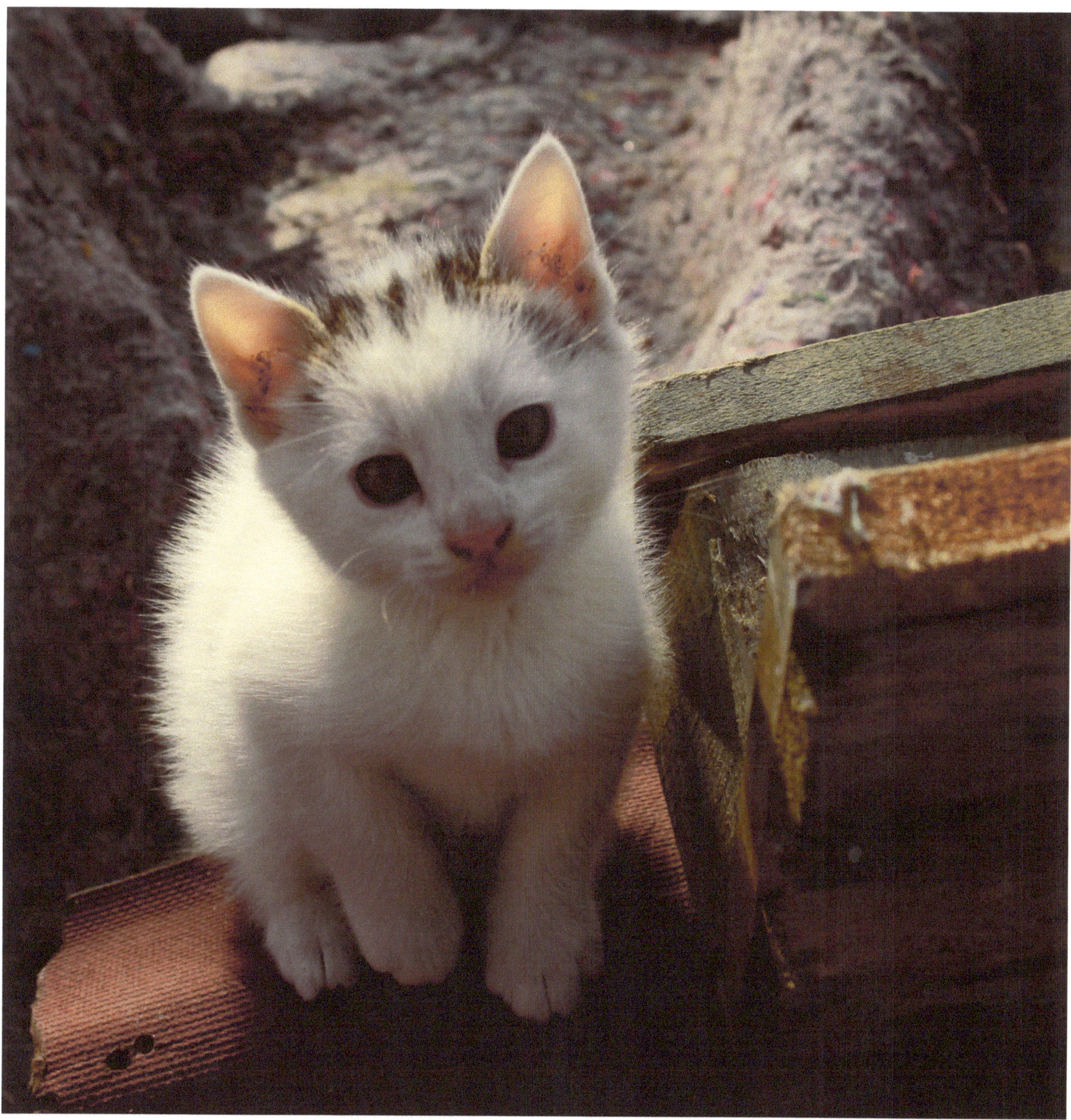

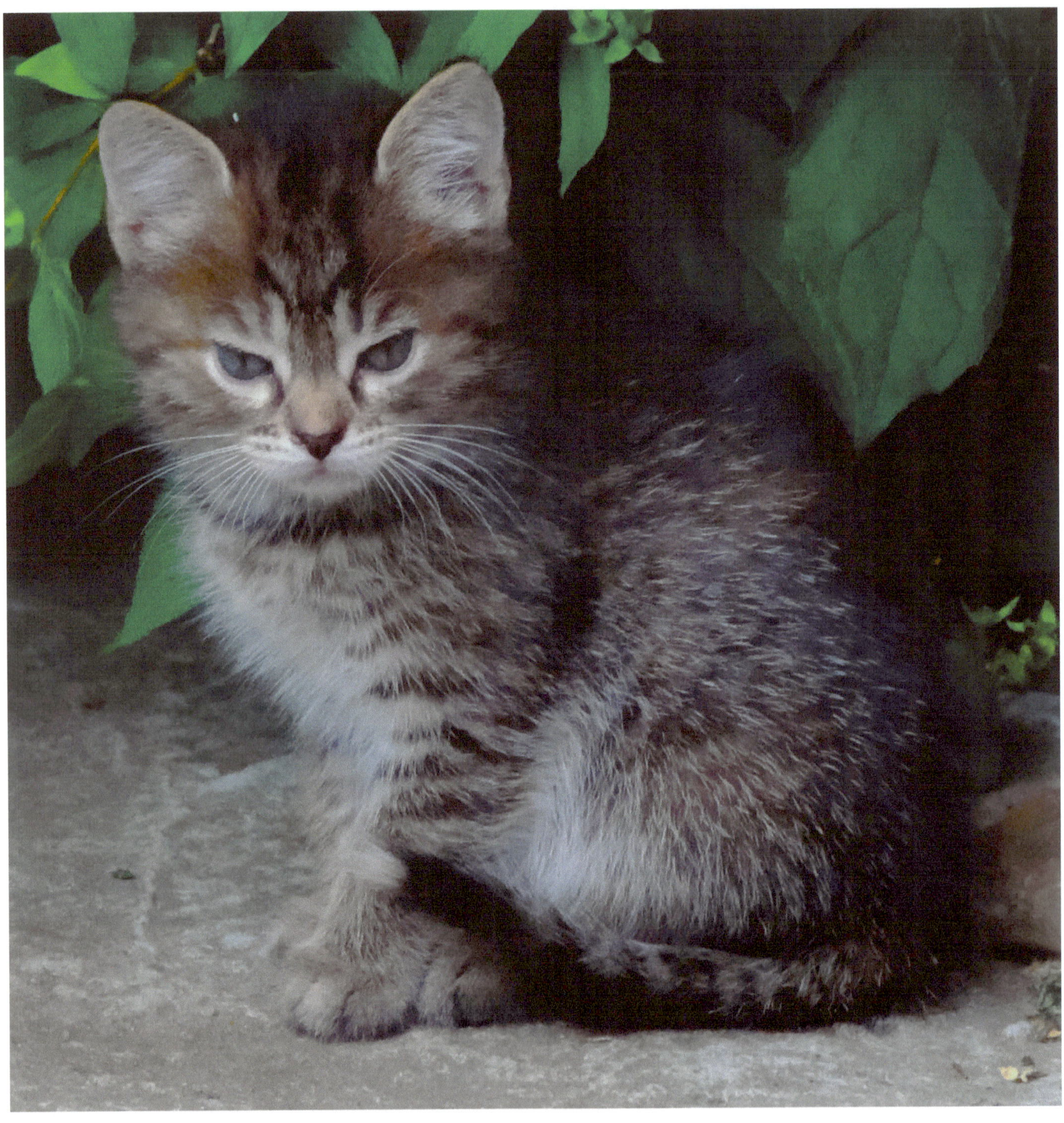

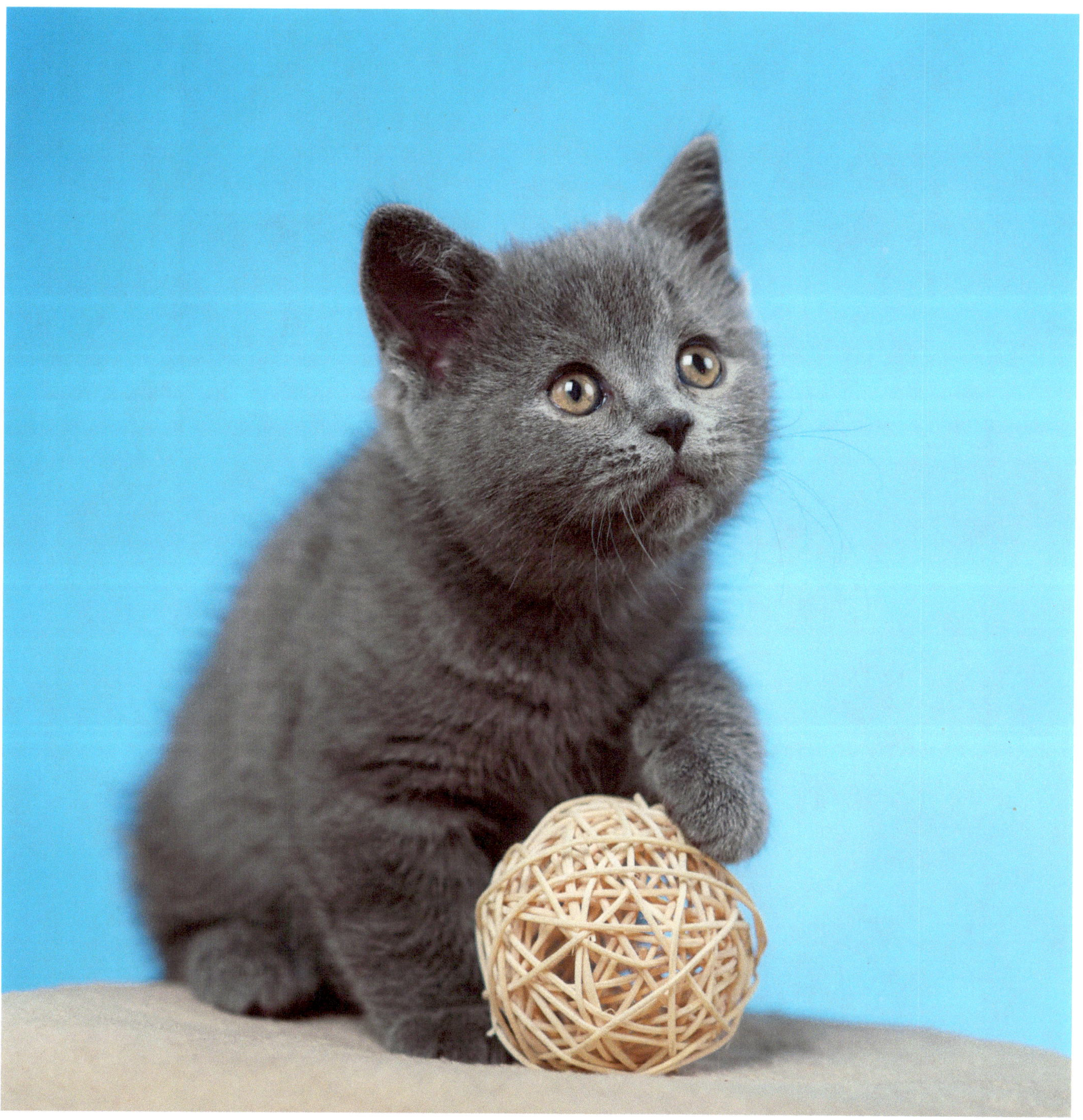

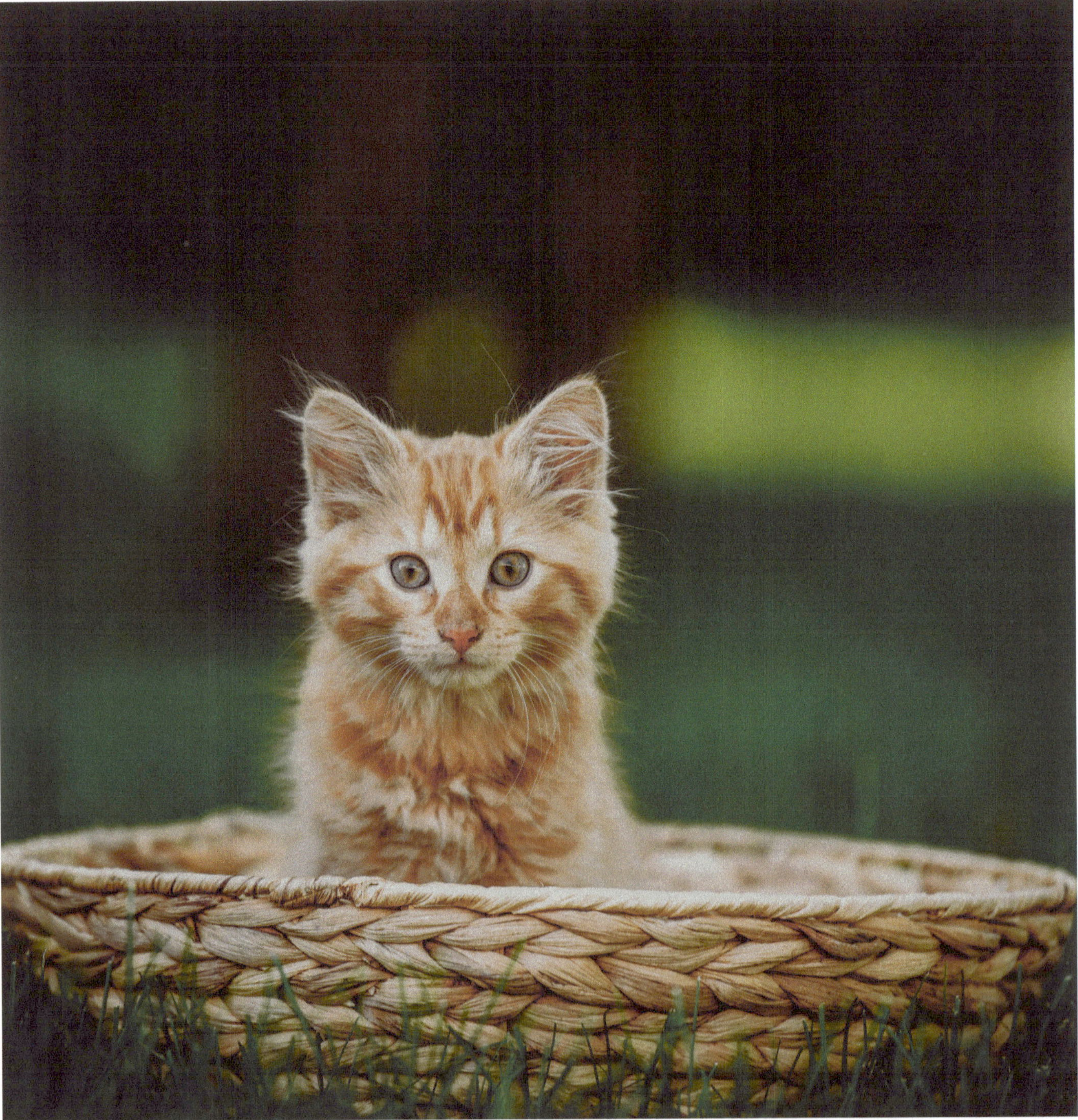

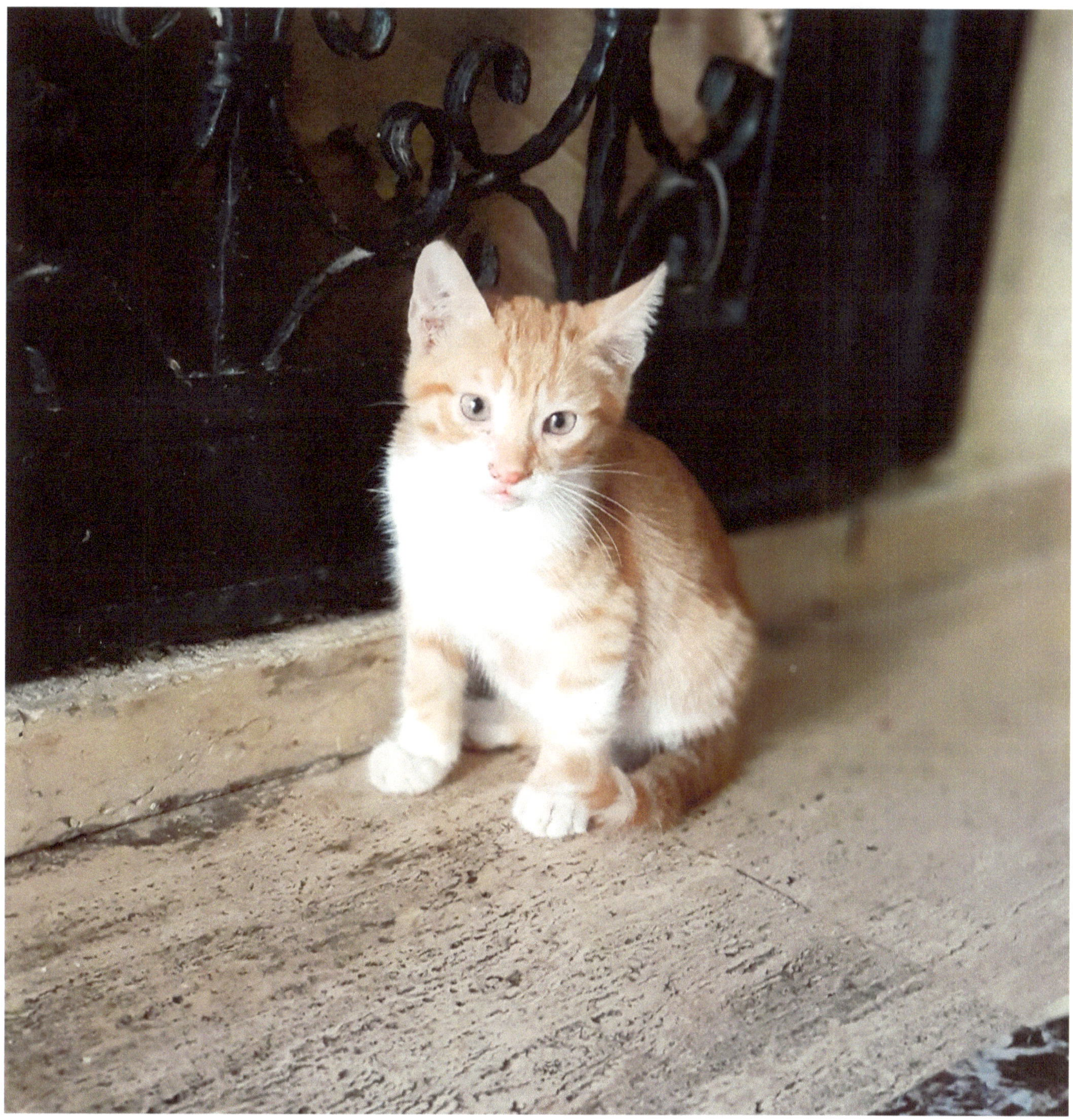

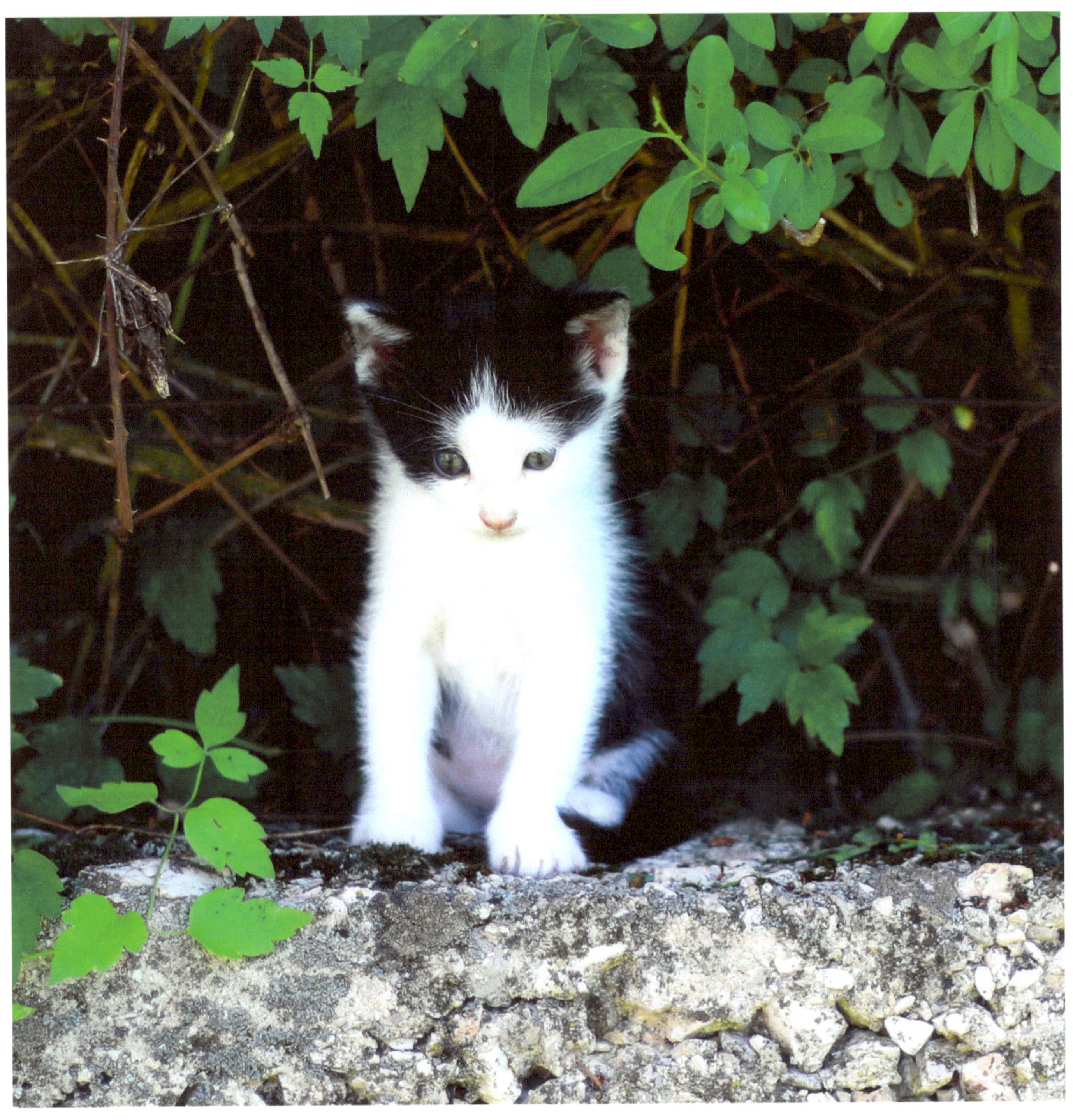

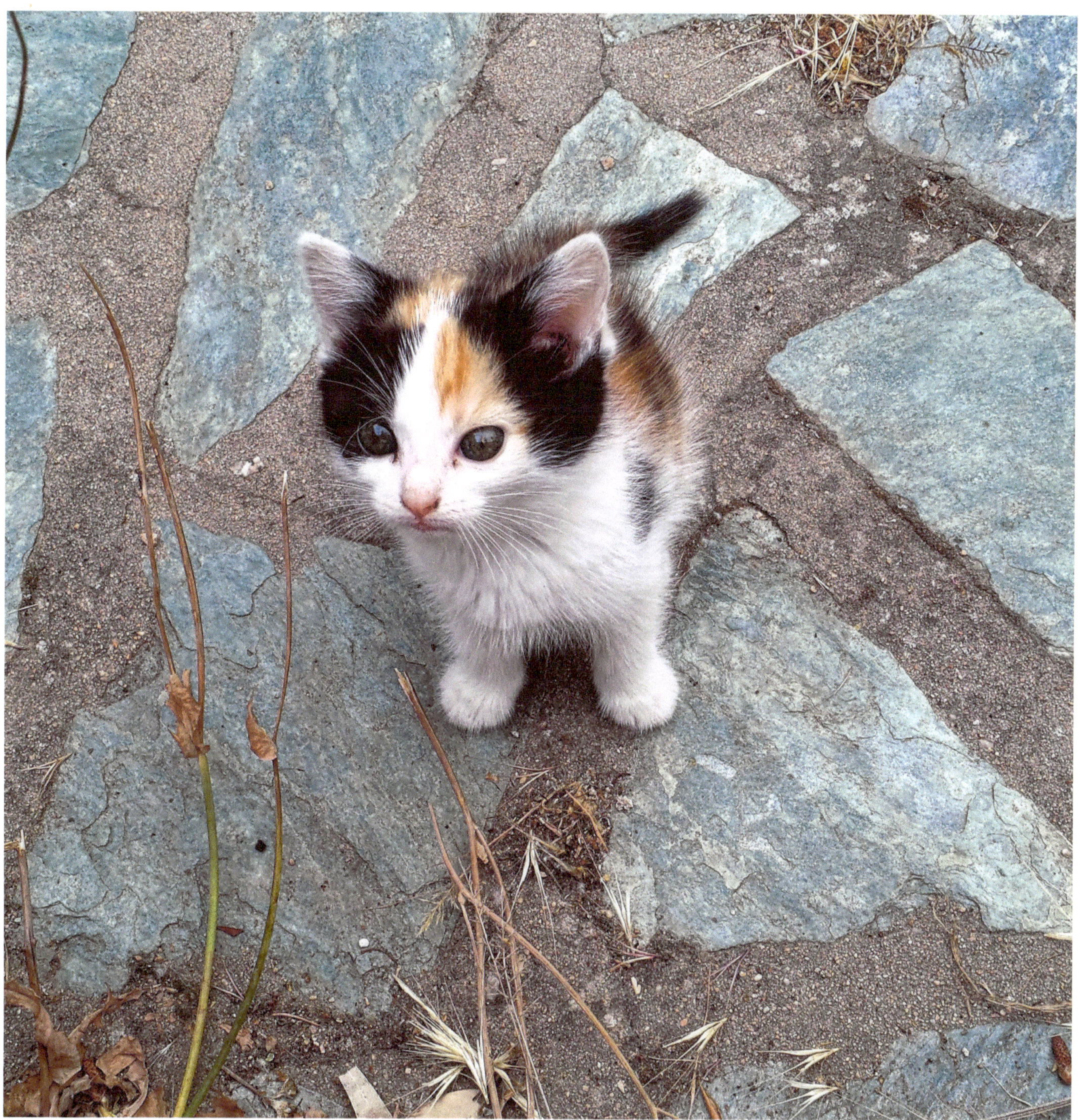

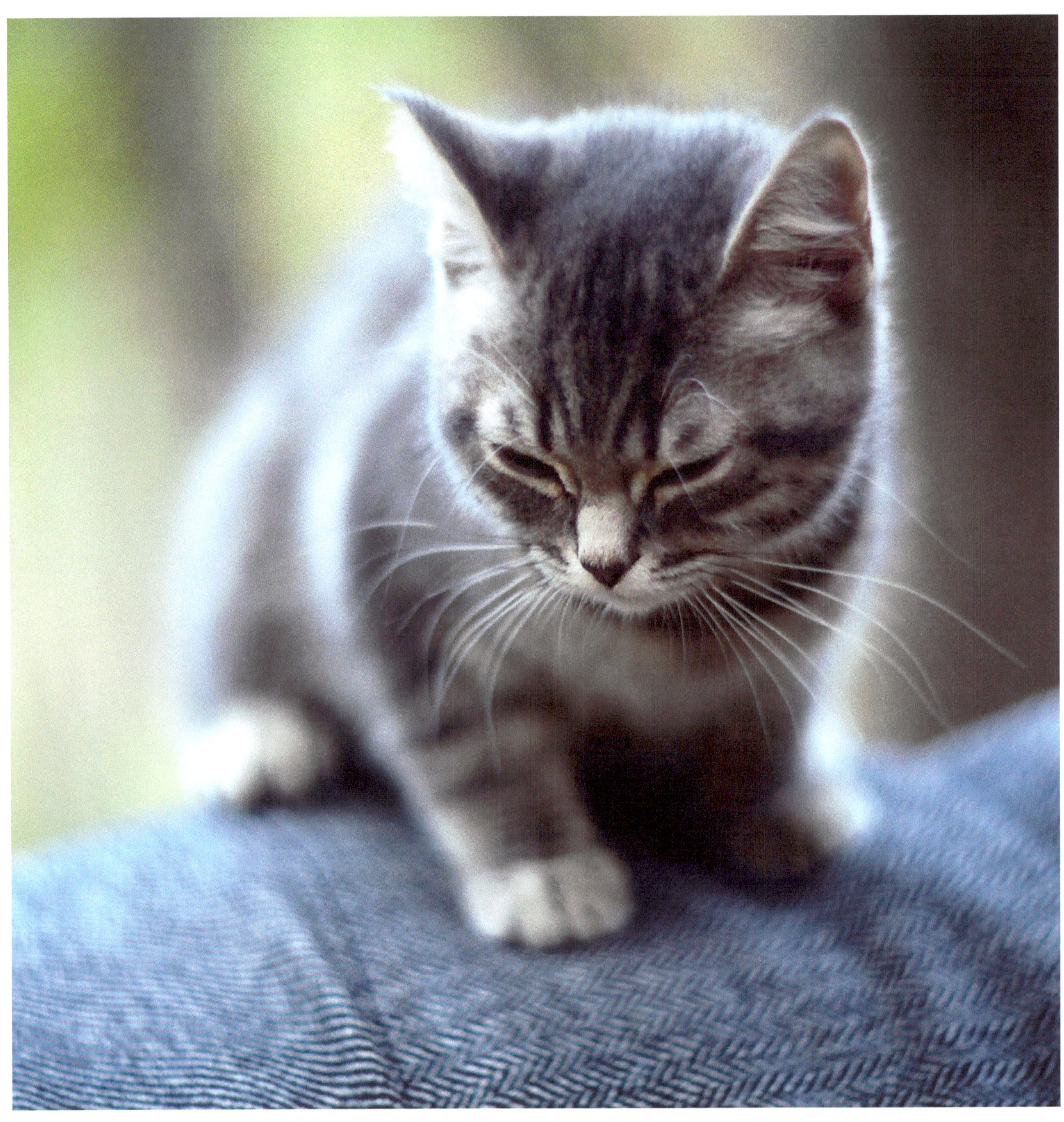

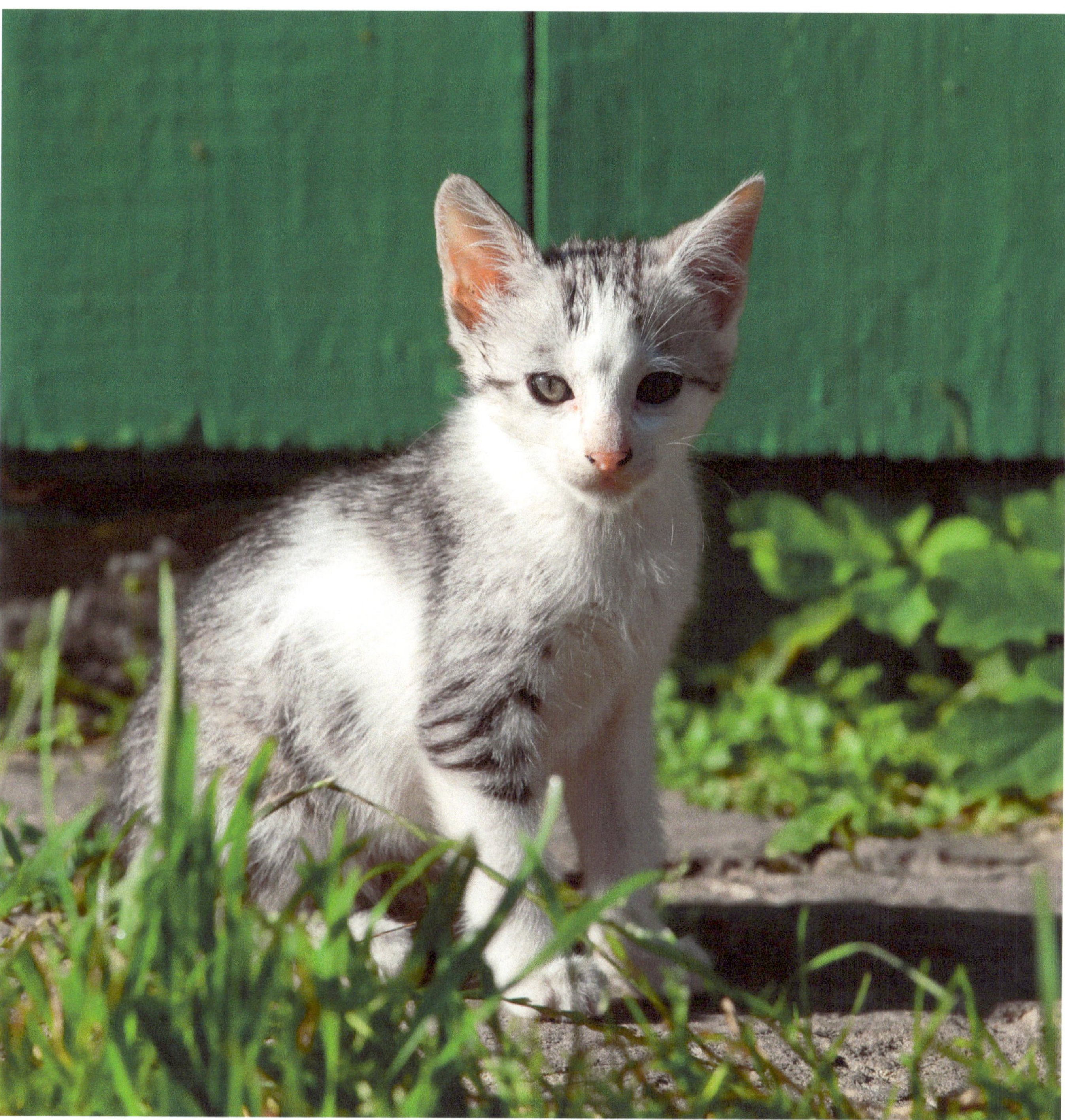

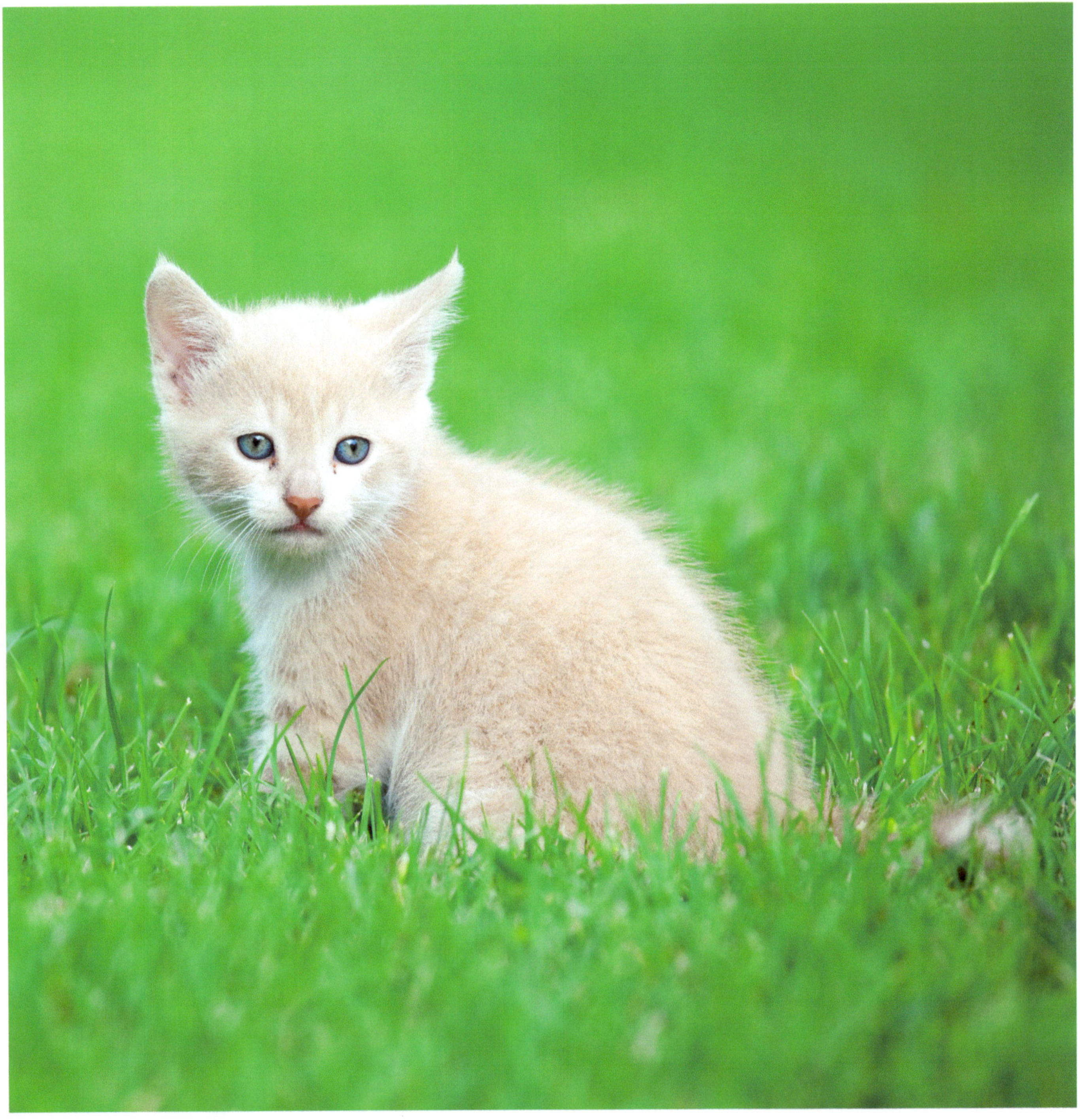

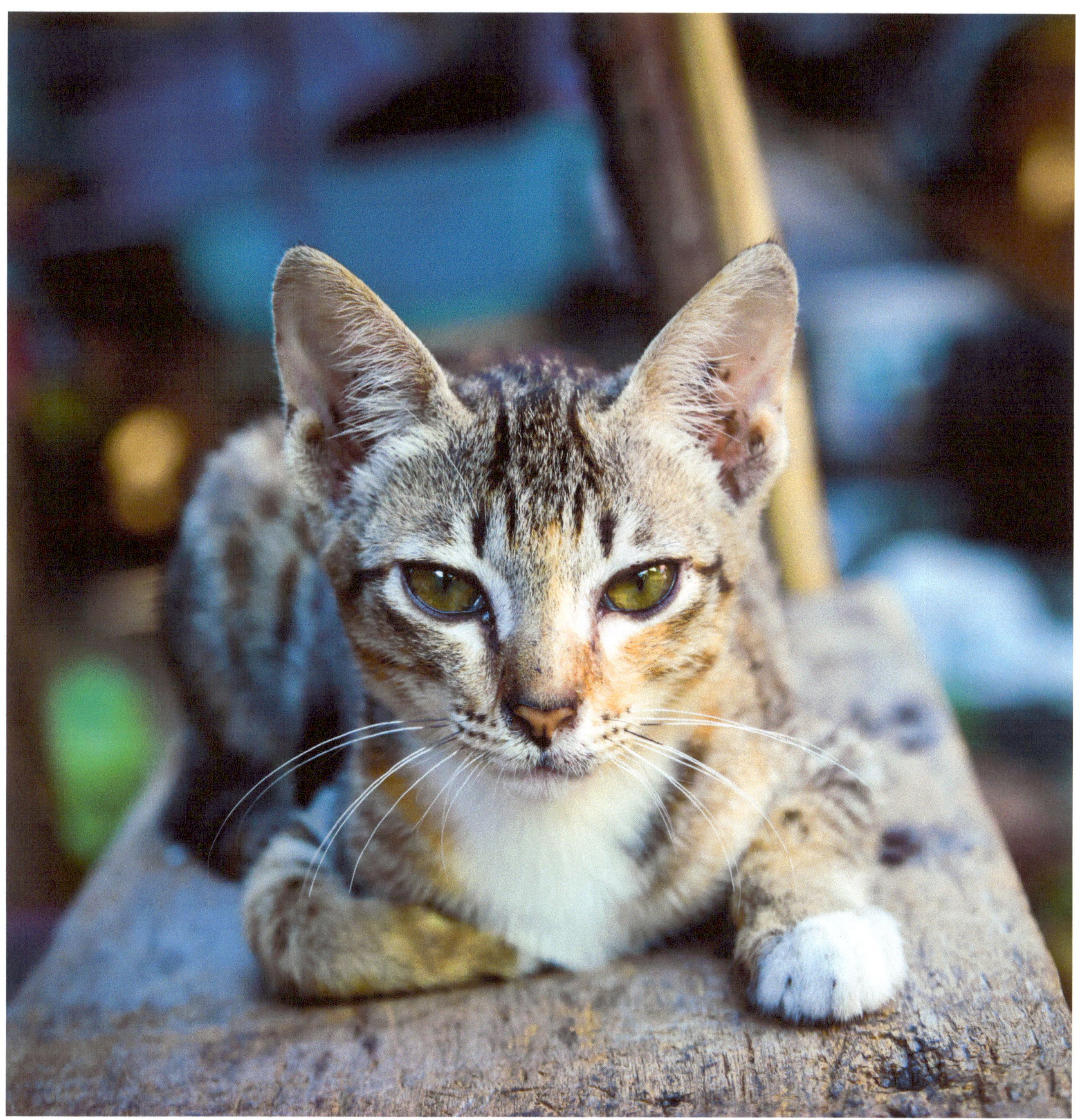

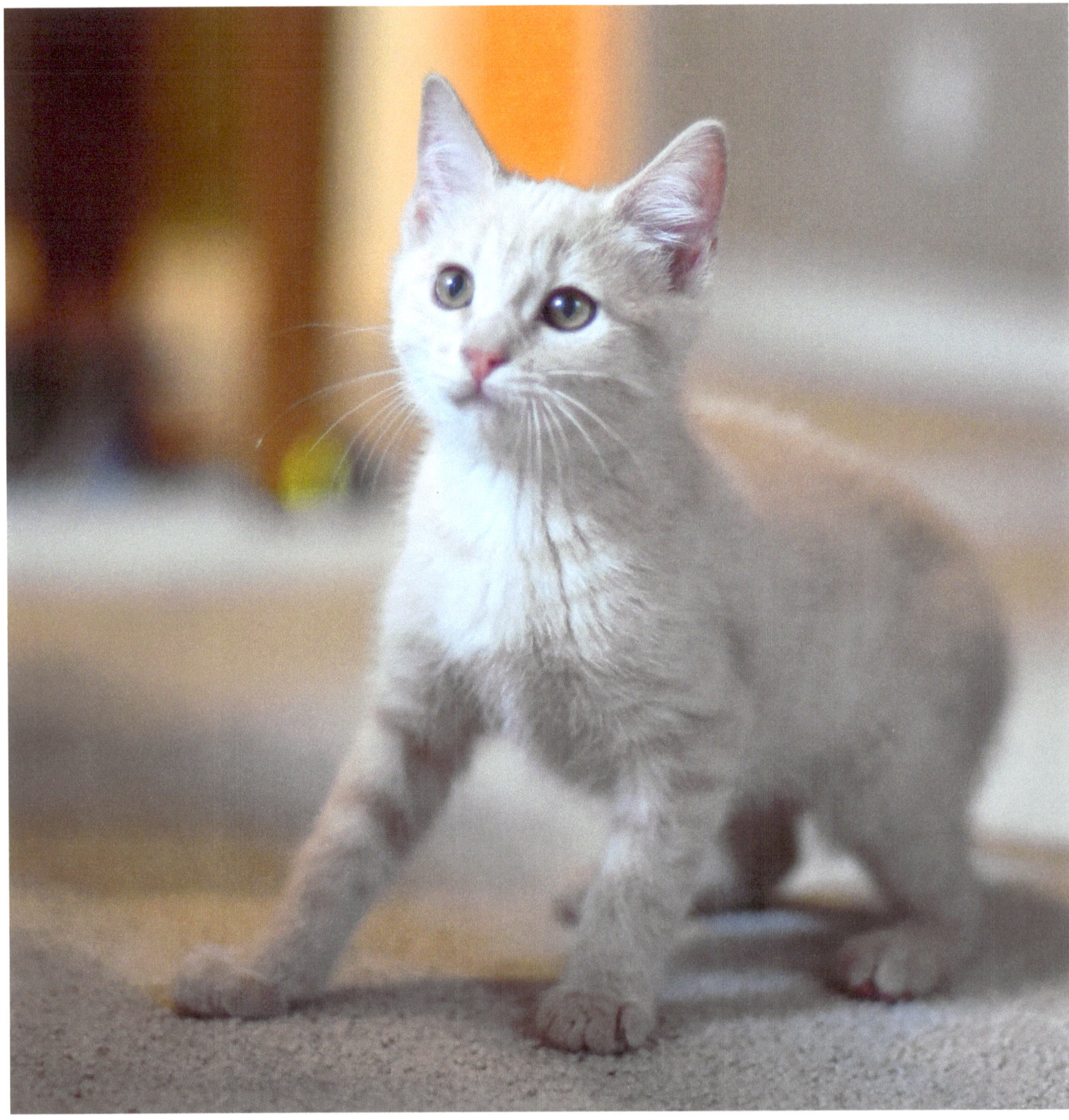

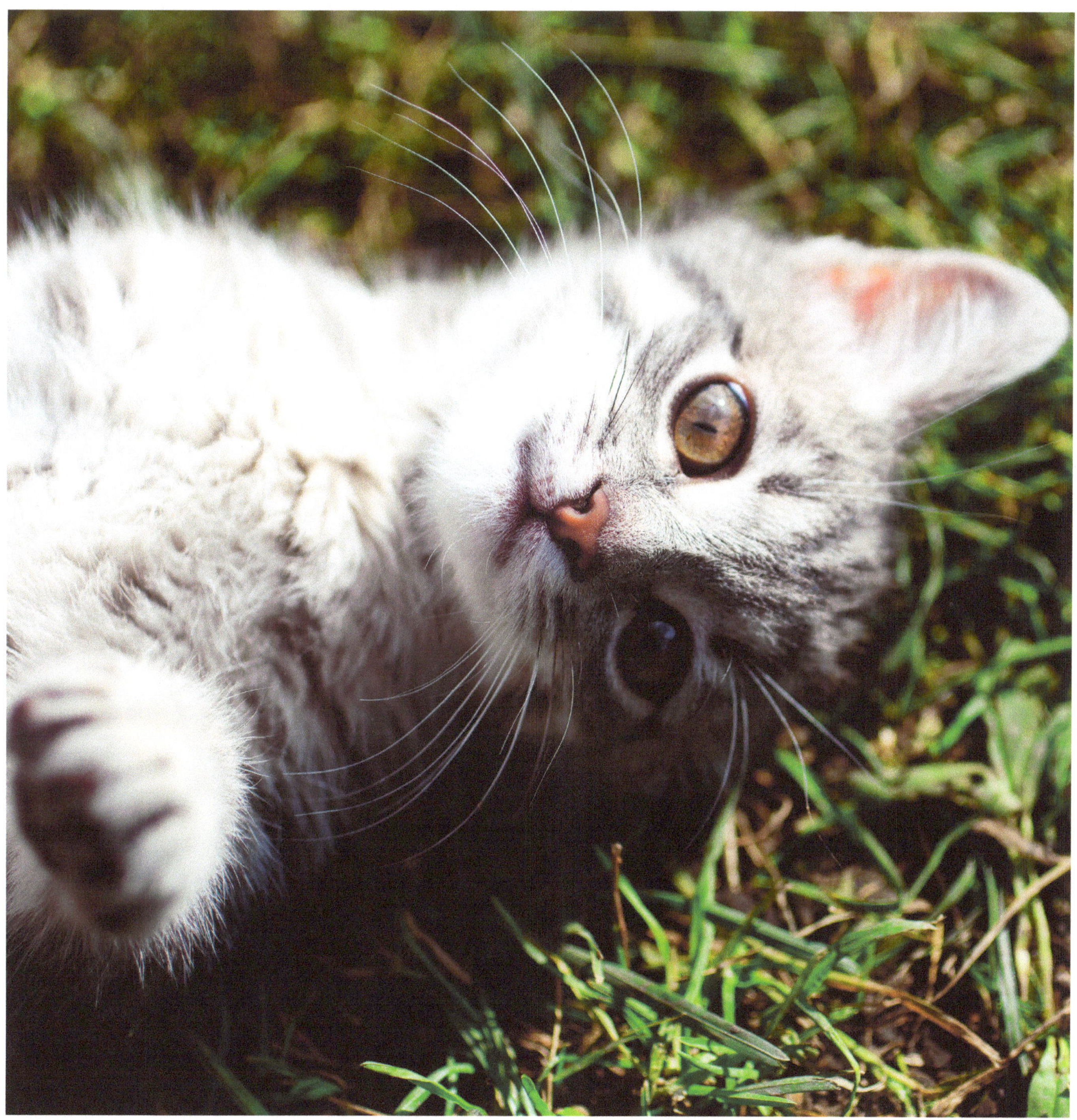

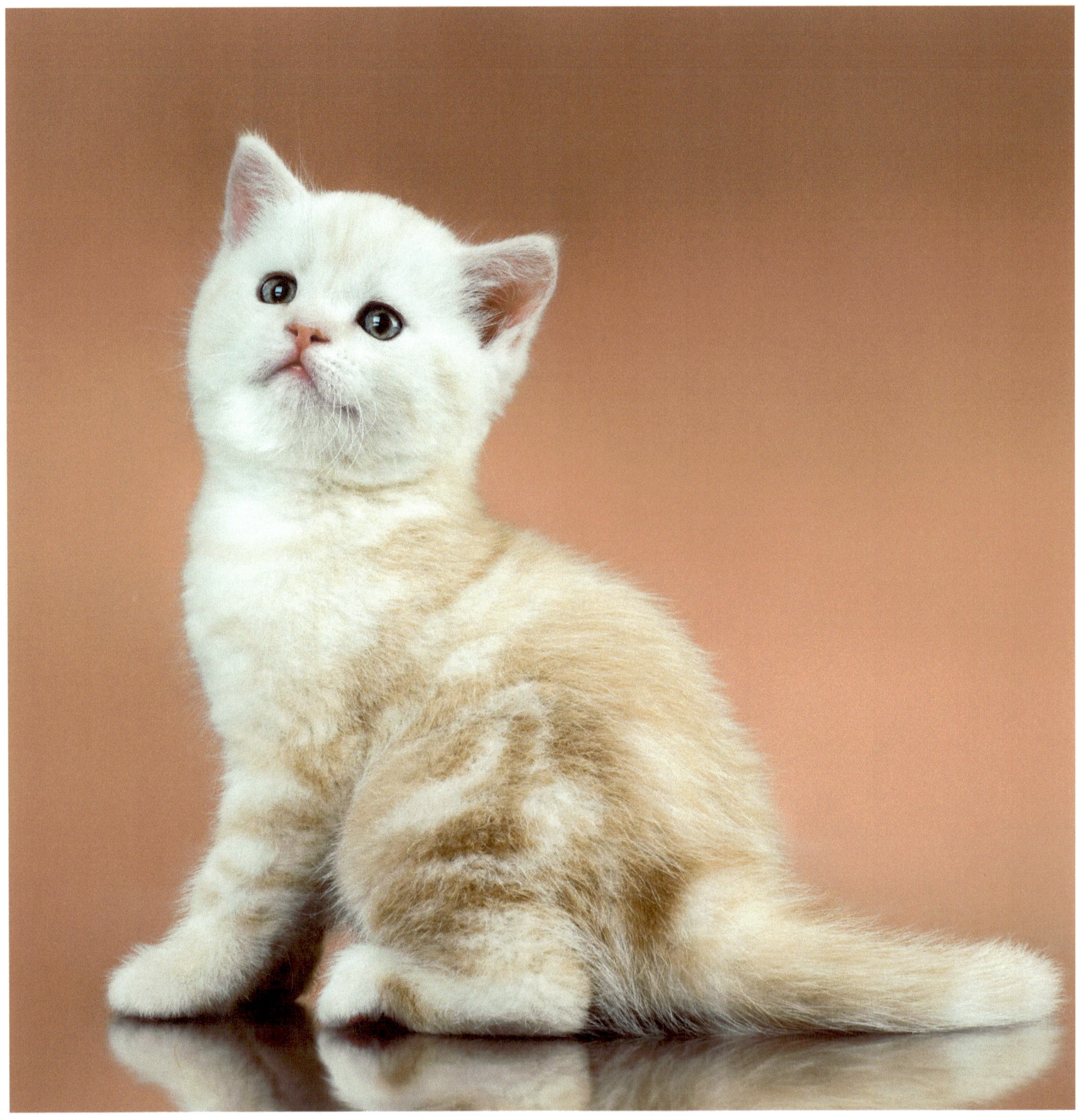

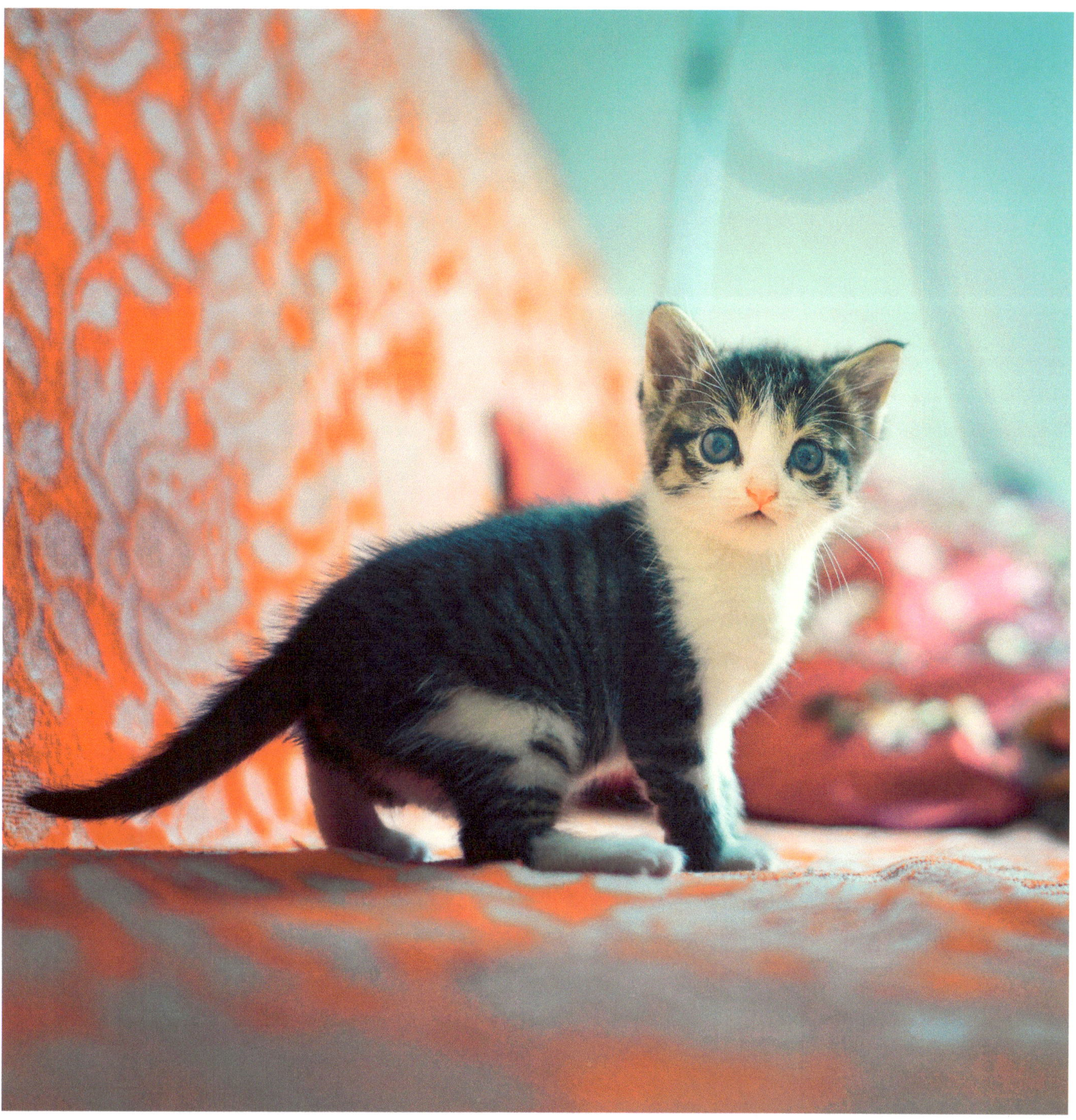

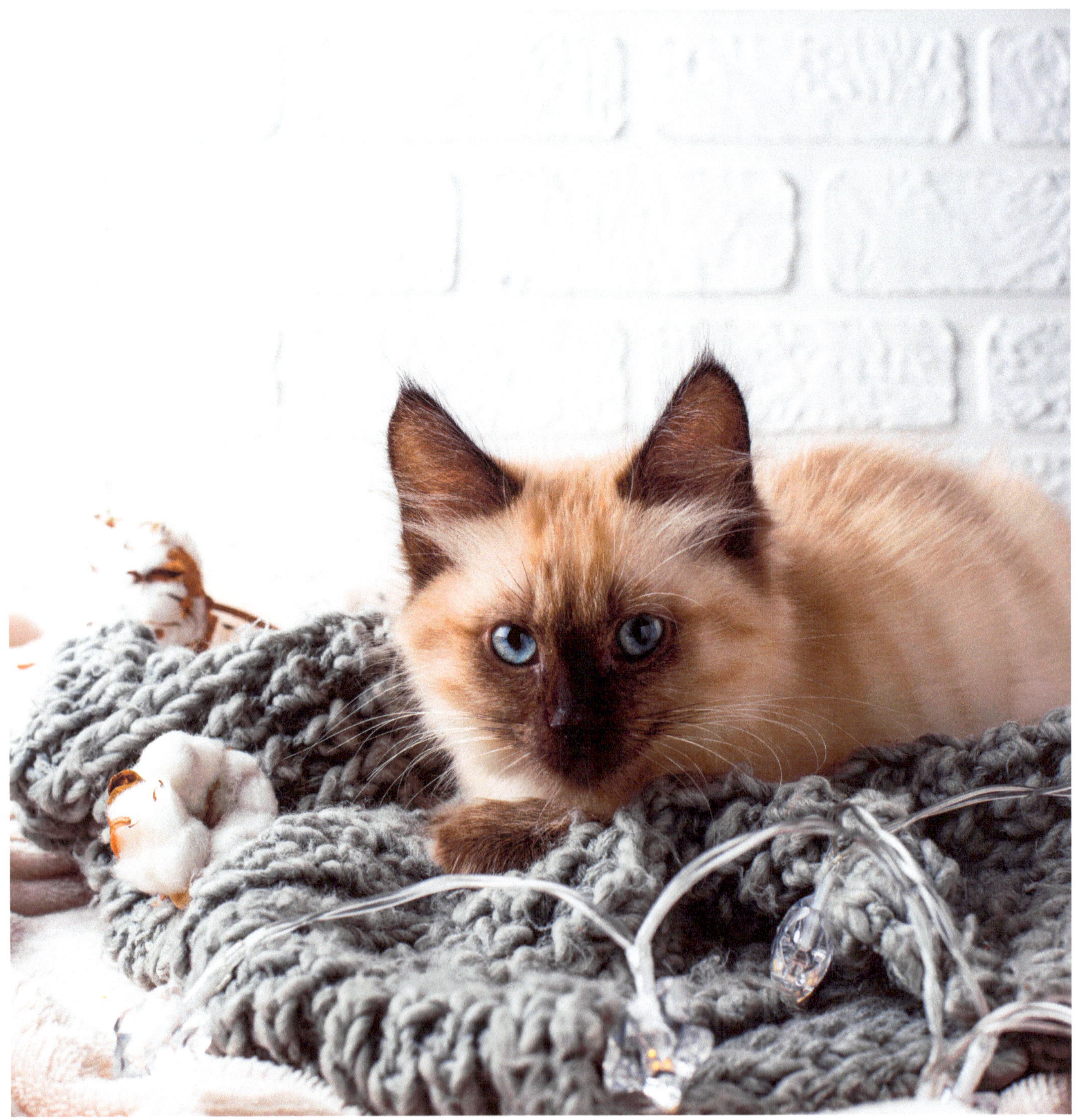

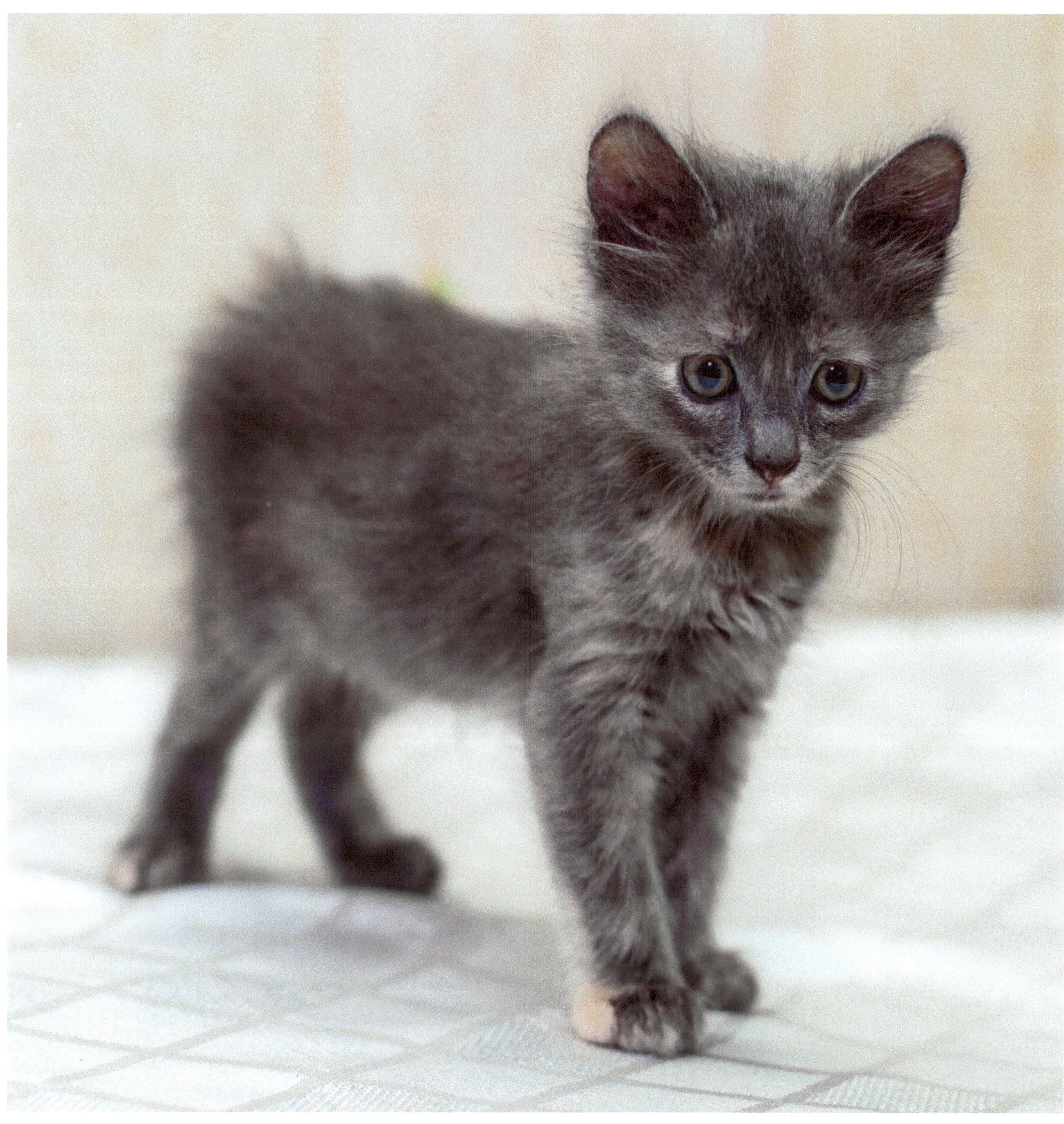

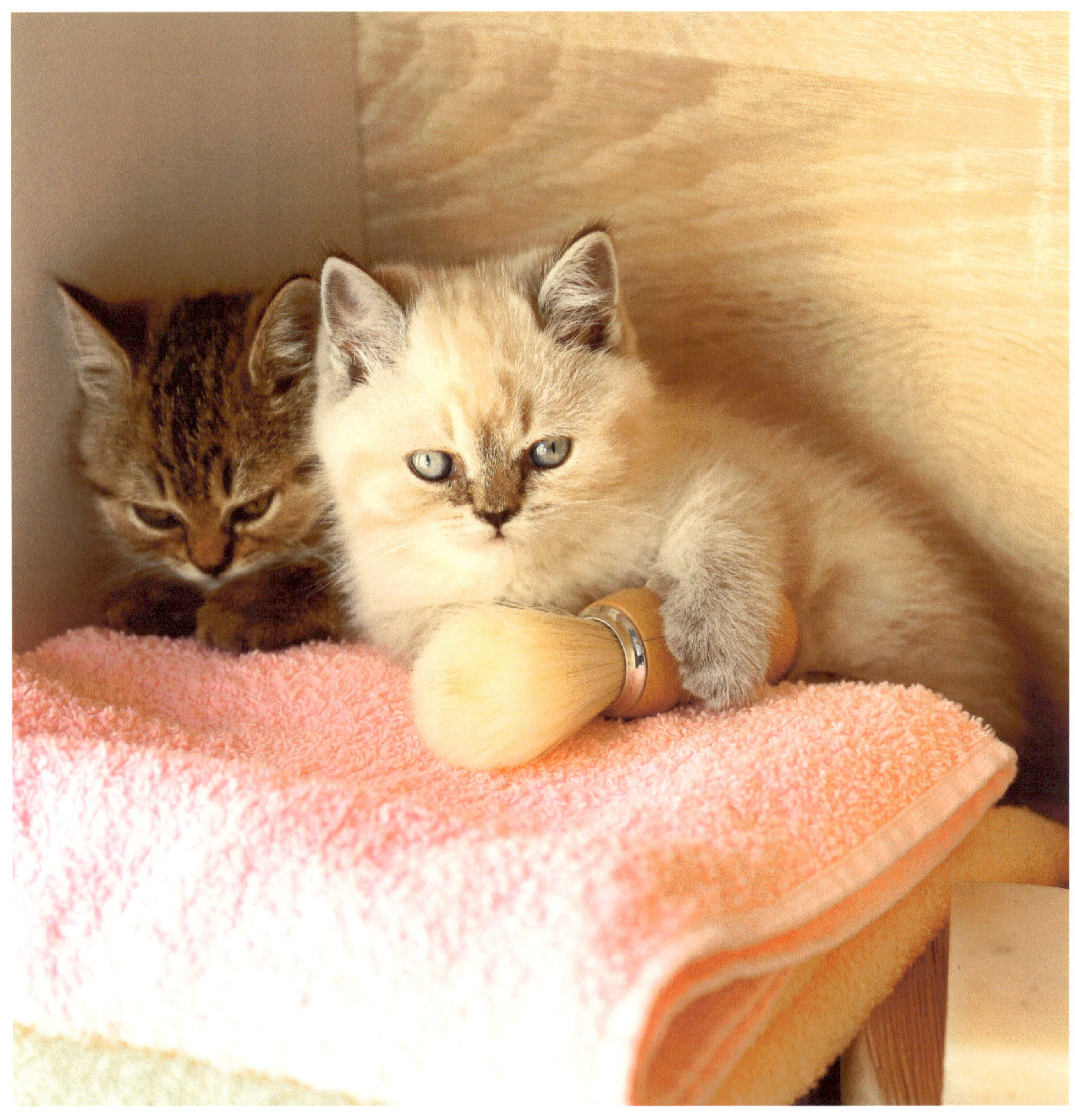

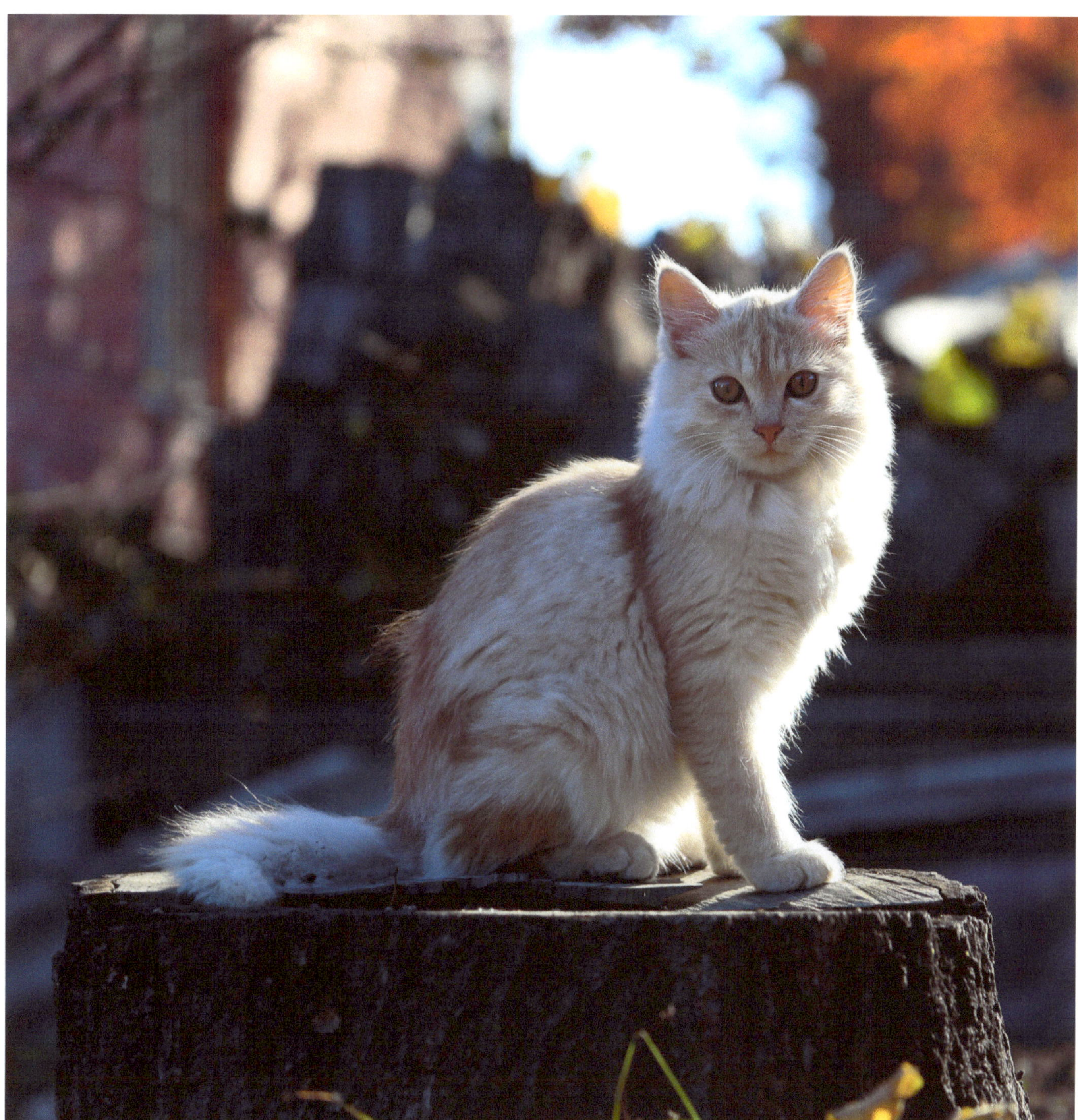

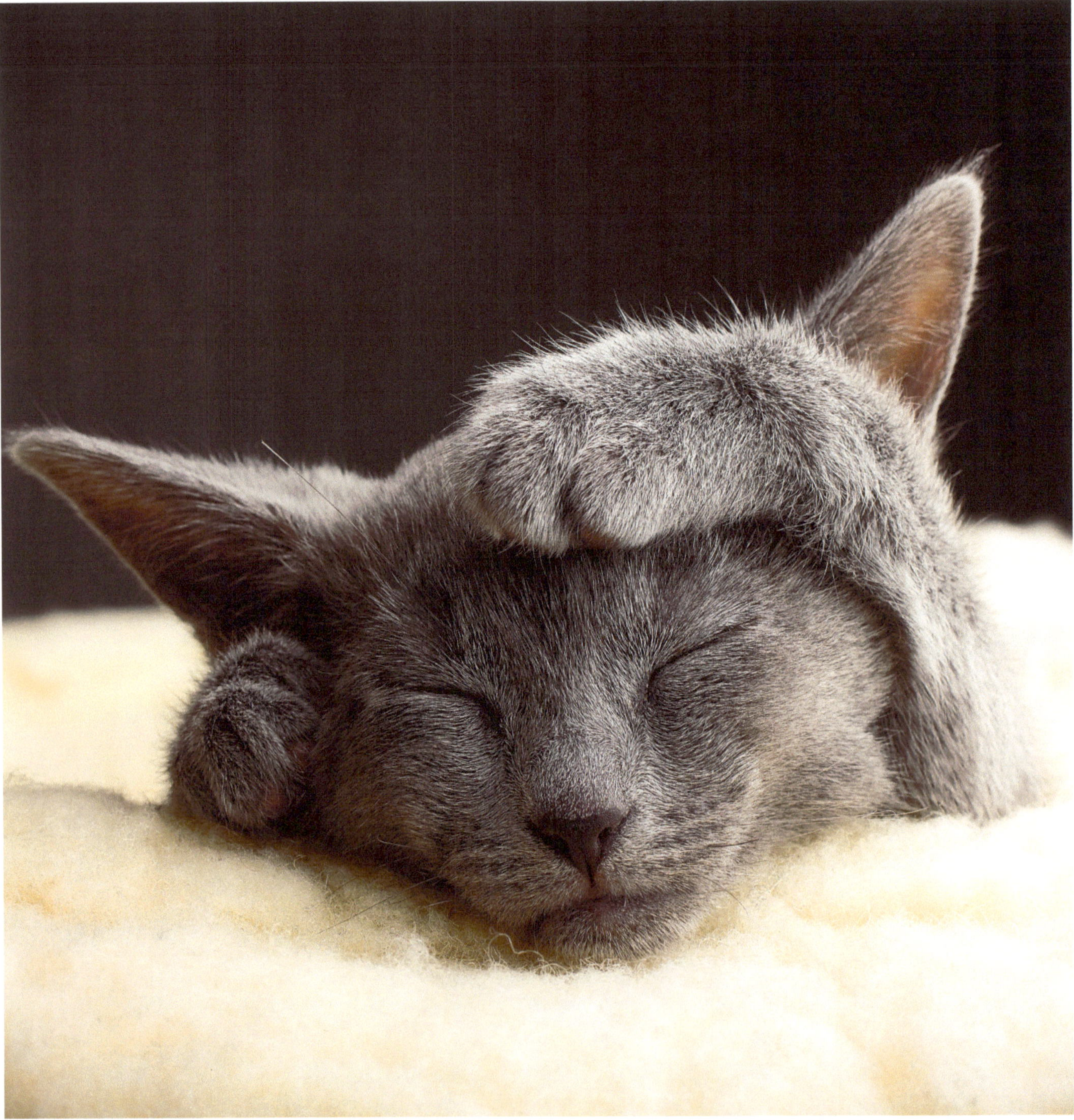

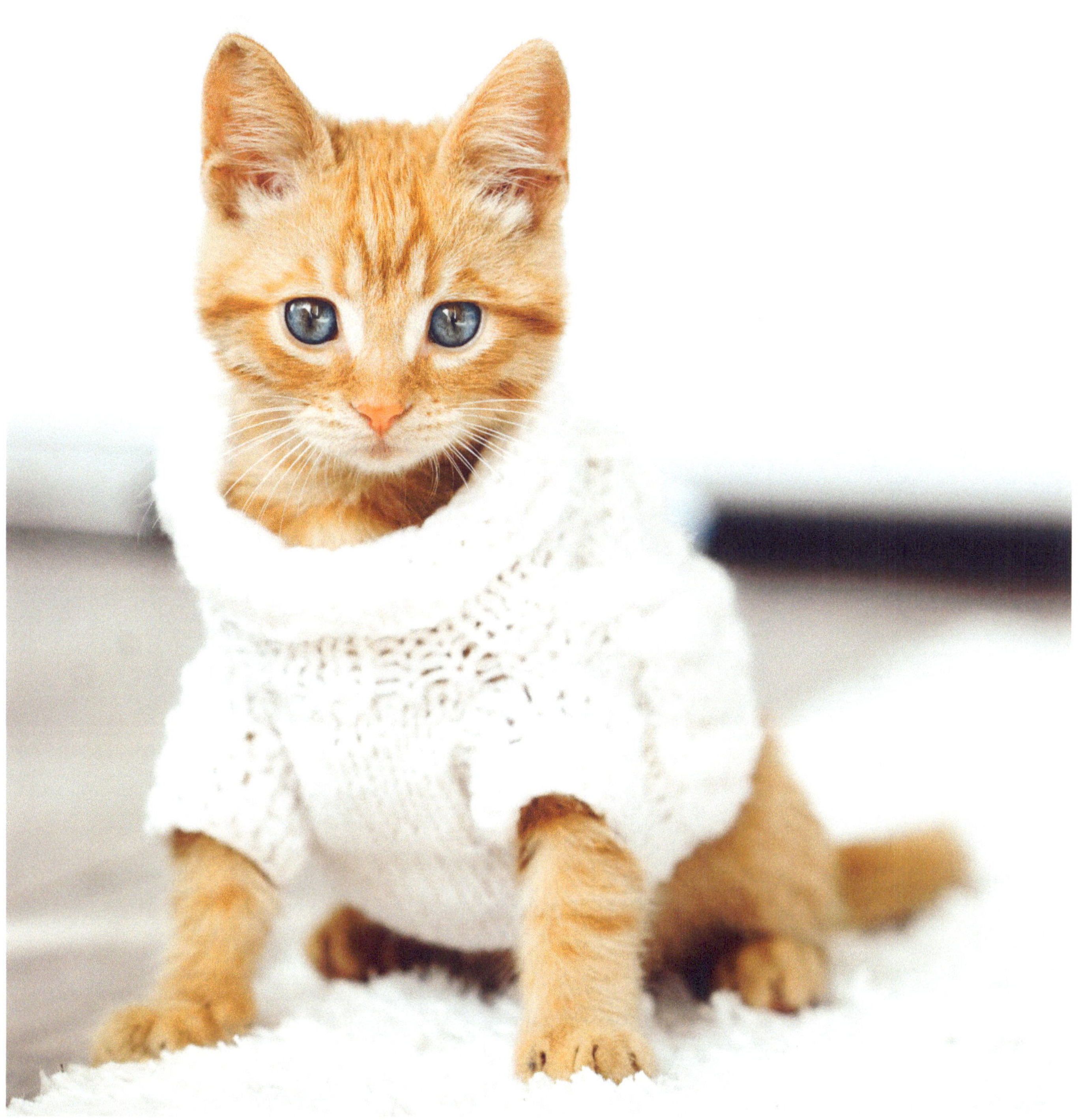

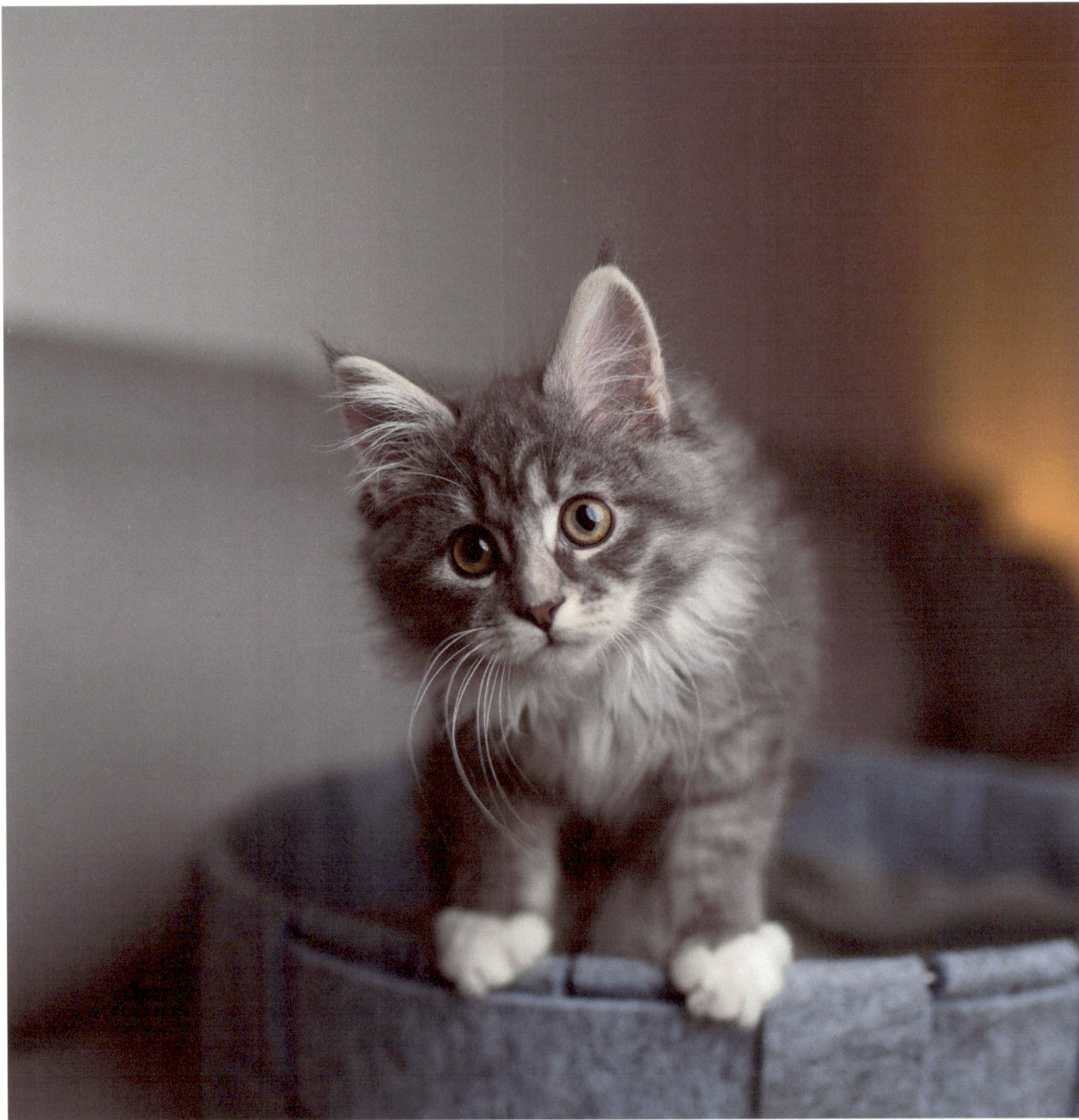

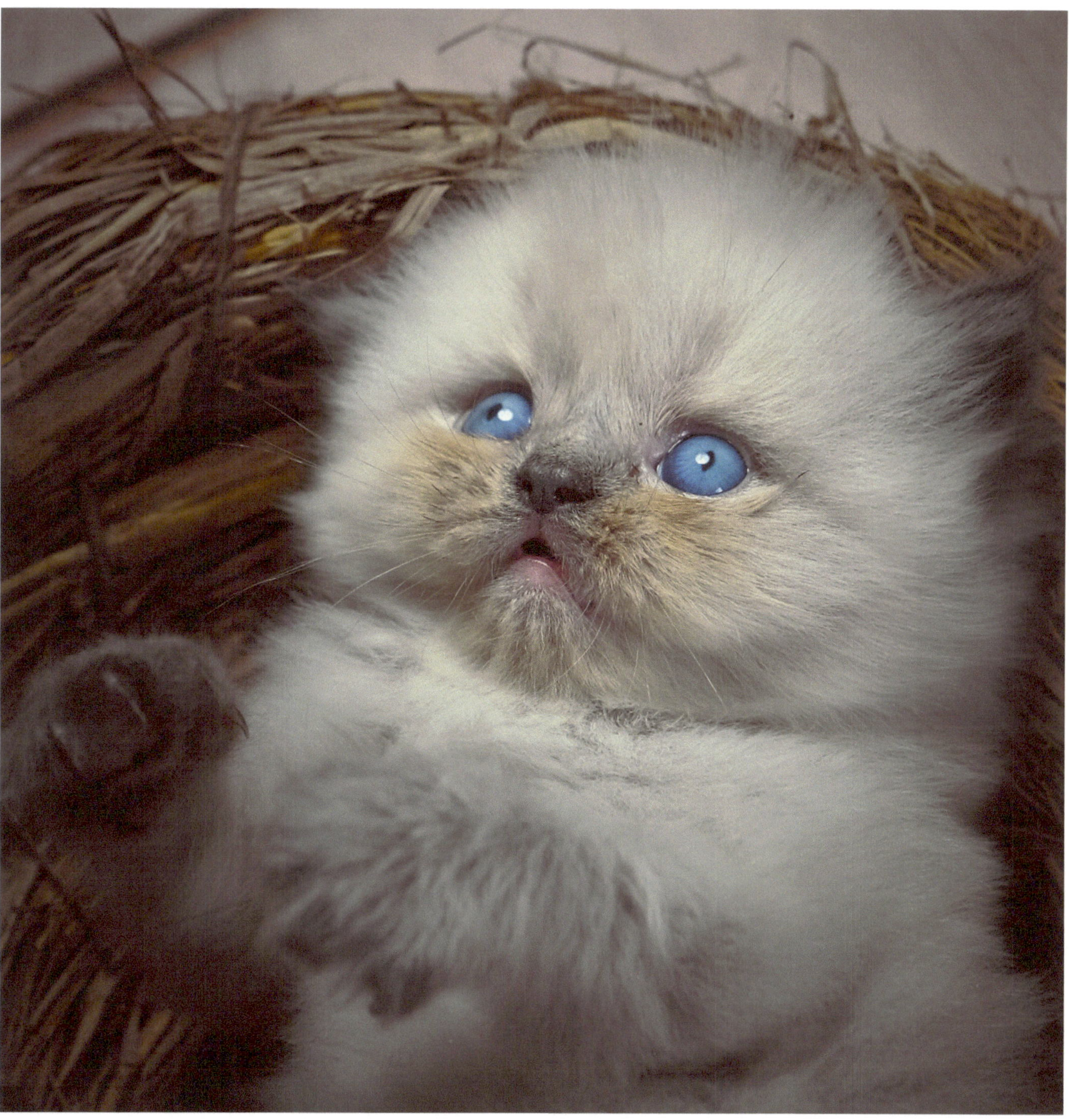

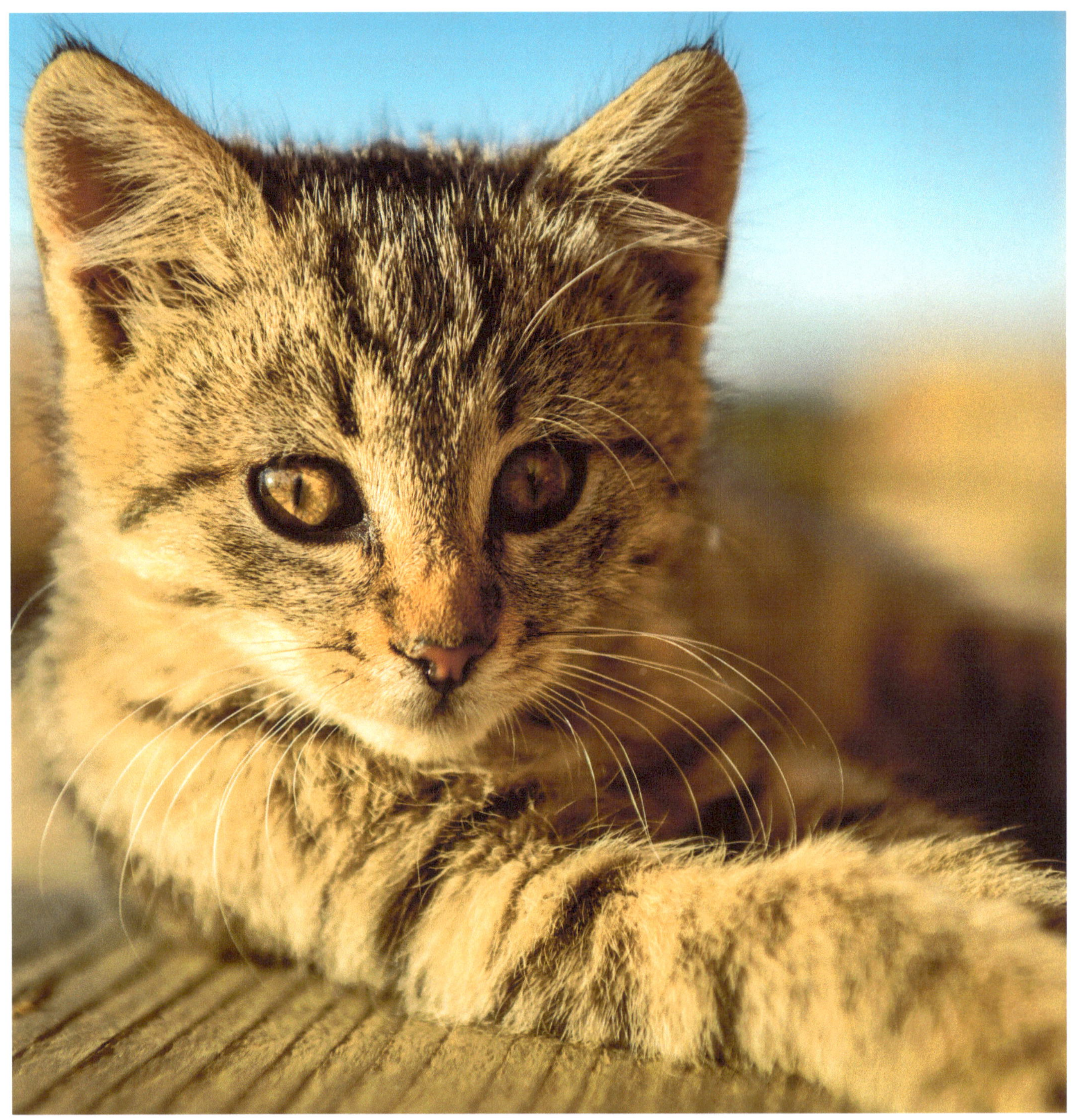

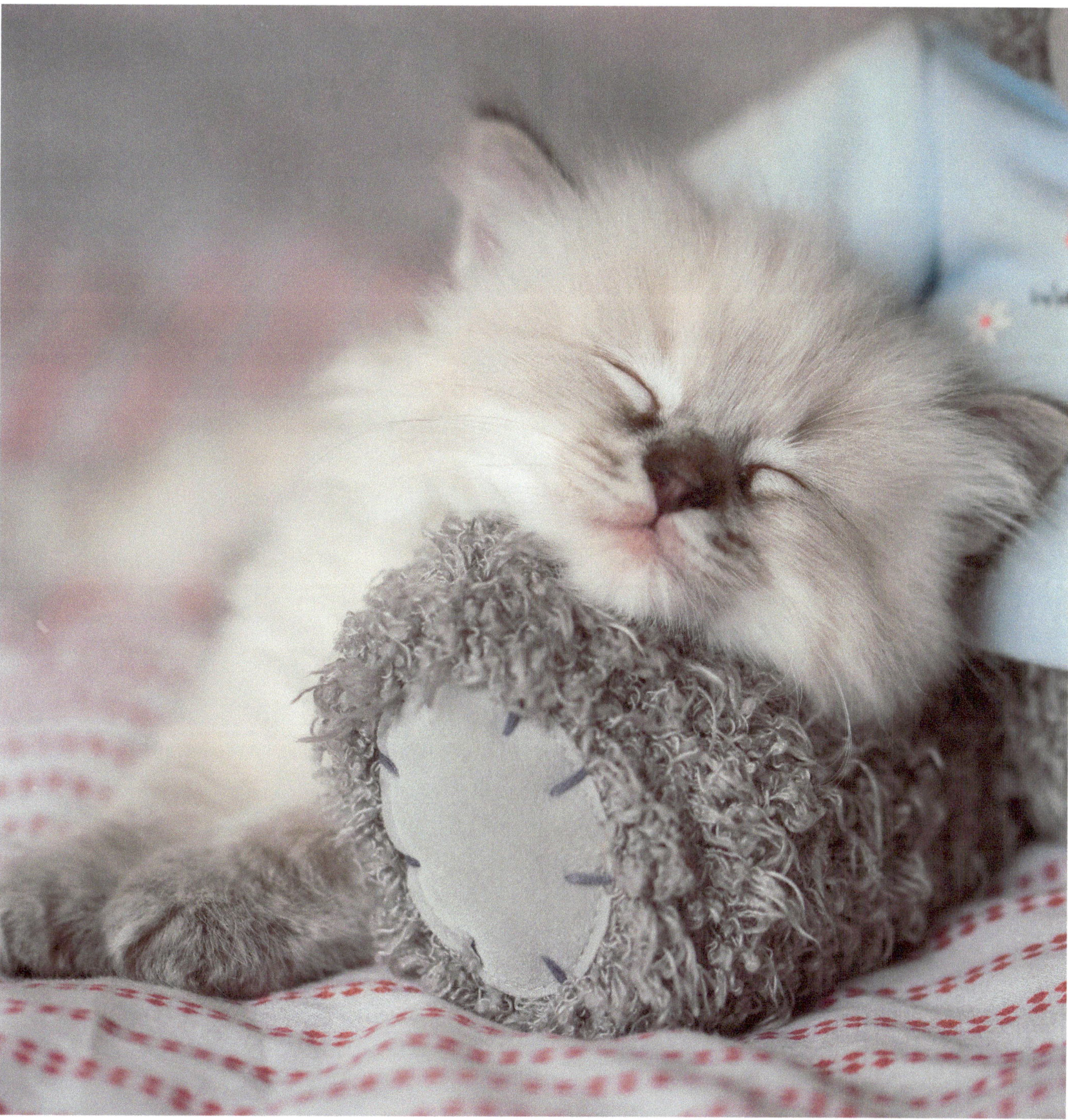

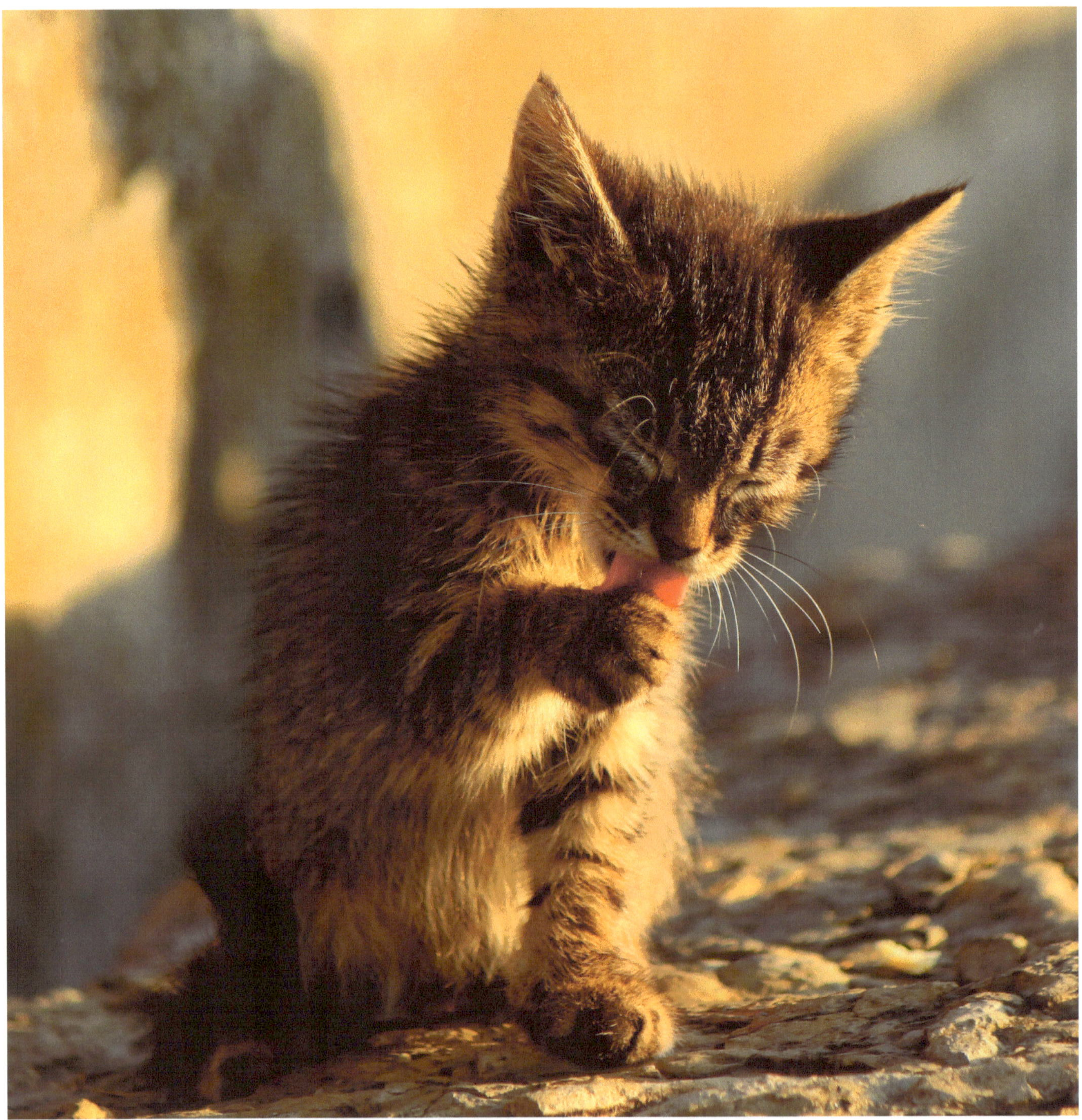

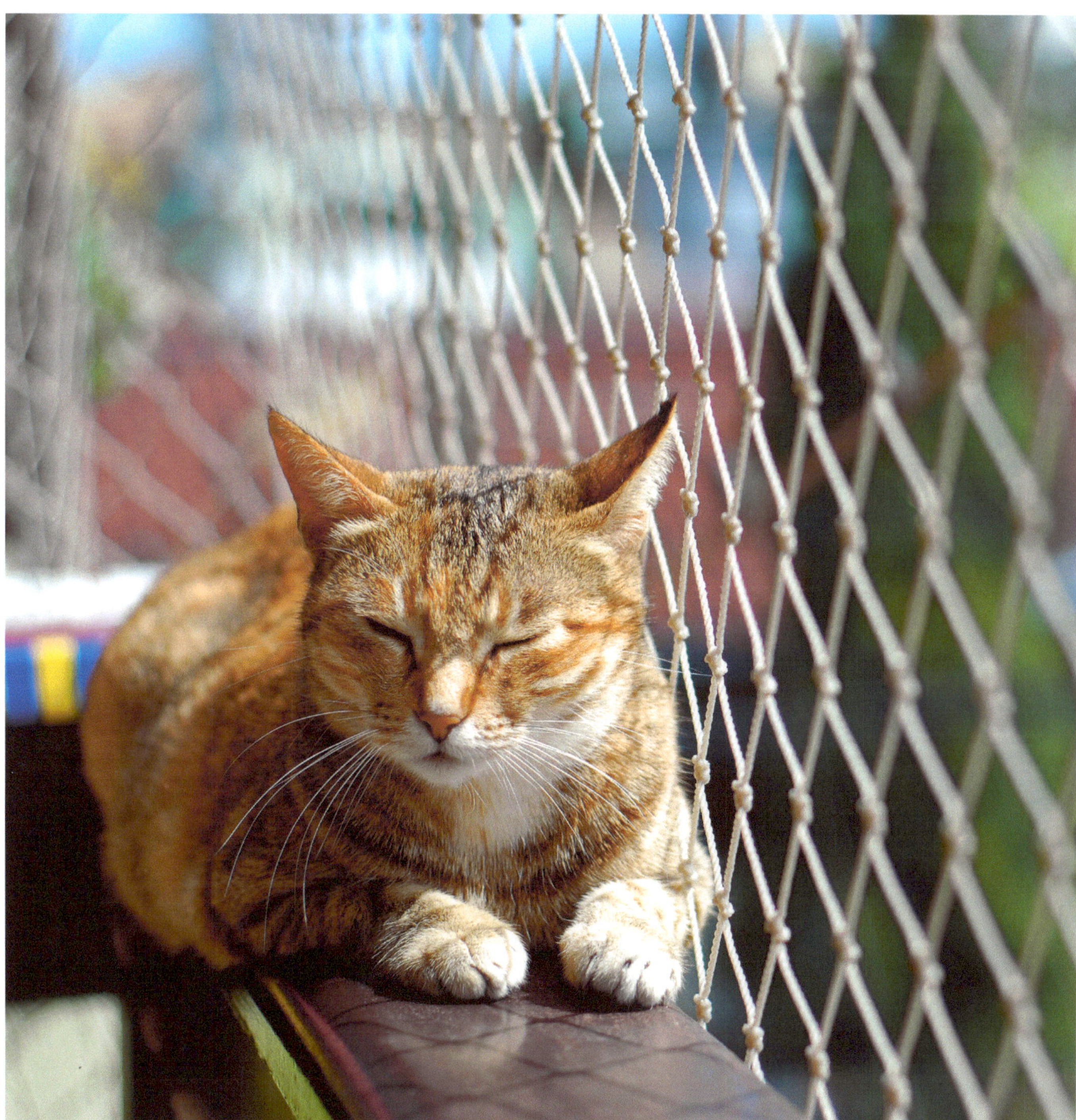

www.ingramcontent.com/pod-product-compliance
Lightning Source LLC
LaVergne TN
LVHW071643180726
843512LV00002B/376